WHAT IF?

DREAM, DISCOVER, AND IGNITE THE FLAME!

A Transformational Journey
to the Life You Were Born to Create

TOMMY TURNER

WHAT IF?
Dream, Discover, and Ignite the Flame!

Copyright © 2023 by Tommy Turner

ISBNs
978-1-954269-03-3 (hardcover)
978-1-954269-04-0 (paperback)
978-1-954269-05-7 (eBook)

Acknowledgments

Each time I write a new book, there are always so many people I can thank. I first want to acknowledge how much I love and appreciate my two children, Kristina and Andrew, and my eight amazing grandchildren; they are my world...

I want to acknowledge how grateful I am for my mother's unconditional love and support. I miss her dearly, but I know she would be so proud of all that I have accomplished since she left this earth.

I also feel so blessed to have great friends who support and love me. I want to especially acknowledge my pastor, Bryan Wheelon, for his ongoing support and friendship. Bryan is always lifting me up and encouraging me to press on and win in life. I want to also express how blessed I am to have a great friend, Ken Elliott, who supports me in all my endeavors. My life is richer because of these two men who have come alongside my life and encourage me to keep pressing on toward all my goals and dreams.

contents

Introduction

When the idea for a new book project comes to me, I feel an extra surge of excitement and life-giving energy begin to pulsate through my heart and soul. My joy and anticipation bubbles over as I contemplate the various ideas and directions each new book that I write will take along the journey to completing the final manuscript.

Okay, I must admit, I might be a bit of an odd duck... You see, I often feel an incredible amount of excitement, joy, and wonderful life-giving energy flowing inside of my heart and soul daily. But that energy flow increases even more every time I begin writing a new book. This extra boost of life-giving energy continues to inspire and motivate me throughout the process of authoring a new book.

I like to refer to these daily reminders and pulses of life-giving energy filled with ongoing moments of joy, satisfaction, and fulfillment as *Quick-Charge* moments. *Quick-Charge* moments like these are an ongoing daily occurrence for me.

If you are unfamiliar with the *Quick-Charge* Concept that I developed a few years ago, I will share the structure of this powerful concept later in this book, so that you might gain access to this powerful life-giving energy as well.

The motto for the *Quick-Charge* Concept is as follows:

Learn it, live it, and inspire others...
Quick Charge Your Life!

Perhaps you may be wondering what any of this has to do with helping you discover your best dreams and living the life you were born to create. Well, stay with me as I continue to work through this thought.

As you peruse the pages of this book, you will develop a clearer sense of what, when, where, and how to move into the life you were born to create, but you must follow a dedicated process as you'll learn about in the pages ahead.

Okay, let's continue to tie in this thought with how my joy and excitement of writing a book can help inspire you to discover your best dreams and live the life you were born to create.

Whenever I begin the process of authoring a new book, I spend hours and hours researching and studying. I often work well into the night listening to podcasts, checking out interesting articles, reading through inspirational books, and listening to audio books.

I spend multiple days, weeks, and months compiling all my thoughts, ideas, and recording my findings. I dig even deeper as I search for appropriate quotes, Scriptures, reading back over past journal notes, and continuing to pray for direction throughout the entire process!

Now, for many, the thoughts of spending multiple hours and late nights that carry into days, weeks, and months of research might sound like an abundance of work. You might even say that all the preparation would drain your energy and joy rather than increase it.

Well, that response is totally understandable. If you are not wired like I am, and if you do not have similar goals and dreams to mine, then yes, the process would probably drain your energy rather than boost it.

I will readily admit that I do expend a tremendous amount of energy, labor, and time into writing each book. But the process feeds my soul and ignites a fire deep within me to continue moving toward more and more successes. I never feel like I work a day in my life, and my days and weeks always seem to pass by way too quickly.

> *"So many of our dreams at first seem impossible, then they seem improbable, and then, when we summon the will, they soon become inevitable."*
>
> – CHRISTOPHER REEVE

So, why do I get such a boost of energy and excitement or a *"Quick Charge,"* as I like to call it, out of the intense process of writing a book?

One of the reasons I get so charged up is because I know that once I have woven all my ideas, quotes, and inspired thoughts together and organized them into a new manuscript, that book will soon be published and, hopefully, add value to others.

However, the main reason I get such a *Quick Charge* of joy and satisfaction when I write a new book is because I am truly living out one of my **best** dreams. My mission in life is to embolden individuals to look beyond their perceived limitations and boldly step into the life they were born to create.

My energy and drive just intensifies whenever I get the opportunity to add value to someone else's life. I get so much personal joy, inspiration, and satisfaction from the process of inspiring others that it energizes my soul.

So, here is the connection to your best dreams and my passions for starting a new book project. My hope is to give you a small glimpse into how incredibly satisfying and rewarding it can be when you are disciplined, continually pressing on, and living out one of your **best** dreams and passions planted inside of you.

Your best dreams and the life you were born to create are just ahead of you! However, you must commit yourself to following a dedicated process along the journey to success.

I have divided this life-transforming material into four key sections.

The first section is devoted to helping you **discover, clarify, and validate your best dreams.** If you follow the process in this section and stop upon its completion, you would only be a *dreamer.* Unfortunately, dreaming of a better life is where most people are stuck today, and sadly, they stay stuck. But with a proper game plan, you can get unstuck!

The second section of the book is about **defining your goals.** A dream without clearly defined goals is still only a dream. You must set defined goals or targets that you are aiming for in order to put your dreams into action.

However, even if a person clearly identifies his best dreams for the life he wants to live and even creates well-defined goals, he often stops before developing the proper discipline and drive to achieve those goals and dreams. Therefore, he must continue and put together an entire custom-made game plan for his journey to success. Fortunately, I have outlined an entire process to help any person in his journey to living the life he dreams of.

The third section of this book will provide you the tools needed to **develop the proper discipline** and a **positive mindset** to achieve all your goals and dreams. However, when I speak of developing proper discipline, I am not suggesting just any kind of discipline. I will show you how to create a very focused and intentional set of custom-designed disciplines that will help propel you forward to achieve your wildest dreams. You will create your very own what I call "Secret Sauce Formula" for success!

The fourth and final section of this book will be dedicated to **determining your drive**. It is important to understand and accept that achieving your best dreams will take an abundance of hard work, focus, discipline, and drive to get you there. So, to keep pressing on is imperative!

This book is filled with powerful insights, ideas, inspirational quotes, and specific tools to inspire individuals to realize their uniqueness, discover their dreams, and thrive in this lifetime.

You will find that many thoughts and ideas will be intertwined throughout the book. I am confident that the thoughts, ideas, and concepts revealed within the pages of this book will inspire some individuals to go on to do remarkable things as they discover their best dreams, define their goals, develop the proper disciplines and continue to press on with tremendous drive to look beyond their perceived limitations and boldly step into the life they were born to create.

If not you, then who? If not now, then when? The time is now to chase after your best dreams and goals. You can rest when you get to heaven!

"I want to be all used up when I die."
— GEORGE BERNARD SHAW

"If you will dare to reach down inside your soul and feel around a bit, you will find a long-forgotten dream."
— LUCAS CUNNINGHAM

SECTION ONE

Discover Your Best Dreams

CHAPTER 1
My Mother's Wise Words

As I began my initial research on writing a book about discovering your best dreams and living the life you were born to create, I felt a bit hesitant about my ideas and qualifications for this project. These hesitant thoughts made me question my confidence and ability to write a book on such a powerful subject matter.

Now that opening paragraph may sound a bit contradictory if you read the introduction to this book. After all, I mentioned that I always feel an incredible amount of excitement, joy, and wonderful life-giving energy flowing in my heart and soul every time I begin writing a new book. I also mentioned how this life-giving energy continues to flow, inspire, and motivate me throughout the process of writing a new book.

Let me explain why I felt so hesitant and insecure at first…

My challenging or hesitant thought was this: when I began doing the research and compiling notes for this subject, I quickly discovered that many authors are far more qualified, accomplished, interesting, and famous who have already authored good books to help people discover their dreams, develop discipline, and find the drive to keep pressing on to achieve success.

So, I asked myself, "Self, why should I even bother trying to add my perspectives to a subject matter so well addressed?" I mean, after all, I am a nobody compared to all those famous authors. As a dreamer myself, I wondered how the book I author could help anyone.

I prayed for answers for several days as I tossed and turned in my sleep with doubts and questions swirling in my mind. I continued to do more and more research on the topic, hoping to find my angle and validate my worthiness to write about something I am living through myself. Finally, after several days of contemplating my ideas and thoughts for writing a book worthy of publishing on this subject, I was reminded of something my mother shared with me long ago that helped to boost my confidence. That thought she entrusted to me has led me to many inspiring moments and continues to help me press on whenever I doubt myself. Right when I needed a reminder, my mother's words echoed in my mind and reminded me once again that I am unique.

Yes, recalling my mother's wise words once again helped me overcome my hesitations and find the courage, discipline, and drive to keep pressing on with this book project. I believe her wisdom will help inspire you as well to keep pressing on toward your goals and best dreams as you read through the ideas and thoughts conveyed in this book.

Now, before I share my mother's words with you, please allow me to briefly offer some personal background about my own life that will help bring some context as to why my mother shared her thoughts with me.

For those who know me, I have made a portion of my living in the piano business. I have been a registered piano technician by trade for over 35 years now. I also play the piano and have recorded a solo piano CD as well.

So, because of my love and passion for pianos, my mom shared a profound thought about a piano with me one day, that has echoed in my mind and continues to propel me on to more successes. My mother's wise words were as follows: "*You know, a piano only has 88 keys, but millions and millions of wonderful songs have been composed using those same 88 keys.*"

Wow! Recalling her profound words to include in the pages of this book gave me another *Quick-Charge* moment! *Excuse me while I wipe a tear from my eye...I miss you, Mom.*

Okay, let's continue with this thought! When I was struggling with my confidence to follow through on writing this book, I was inspired once again to rise to the challenge and gain the courage to continue with this project as I recounted my mother's inspiring words.

As I already mentioned, I can acknowledge that many others far more accomplished and famous than me have already offered their perspectives on finding your dreams, developing discipline, pressing on, and achieving success through the books they have authored. However, I can choose or better said, I MUST choose to believe that there will always be room for one more song or, in this case, *one more book* to help inspire others to chase after their best dreams.

Yes, although I may not be as famous or successful as some others, and I may even use similar "keys" that are based on the same subject matters. I believe that my song, sorry, *my book*, will carry a slightly different tune than anyone else's message!

I choose to believe that the thoughts and ideas conveyed in this book will find others who are still searching and help inspire them to discover their best dreams, develop the proper disciplines, and determine the drive needed to live the life they were born to create.

As I continue to chase after my goals and best dreams in life and write more books, I am certain that most of the books

I write will probably be on similar topics that have already been covered by many others. I choose to believe that my books will play a slightly different melody in the minds and hearts of my readers than all the other books written by others on this subject matter.

> *"If there's a book that you want to read, but it hasn't been written yet, then you must write it."*
> — TONI MORRISON

My hope is that the ideas and thoughts conveyed within the pages of this book will strike a chord that propels my readers to great success. Hopefully, this book will play a symphony of thoughts and ideas that someone needed to hear in order to fine-tune his or her direction in life. Then that person can finally move forward to living his or her BEST dreams.

I want you to hear and see the message of why I am so inspired and choosing to press on with writing this book:

It does not matter if others have similar ideas and or dreams to yours.

Why? Because Your Dreams Matter!

It does not matter if someone else's ideas and thoughts seem better than yours.

Why? Because Your Dreams Matter!

It does not matter if you feel you do not have as much talent or as much to offer.

Why? Because Your Dreams Matter!

*It does not matter if you are rich or poor,
young or old, accomplished or not.*

Why? Because Your Dreams Matter!

If you have a fire burning deep inside your heart and soul to do something that will add value to others, then your dreams matter! You are unique! When you discover your BEST dreams inside your heart and soul, then go after them because the world is waiting!

Your best dreams and passions are unique to YOU and to YOU alone. There will always be room for one more *song*... I hope my mother's wise words will also inspire you to discover your best dreams, realize your uniqueness, keep pressing on, and thrive in this lifetime. Indeed, the time is now for you to realize your uniqueness, discover your dreams, and thrive in this lifetime.

> *"Many of life's failures are people who did not realize how close they were to success when they gave up."*
> – THOMAS A. EDISON

CHAPTER 2
There is More to the Story

When it comes to discovering your best dreams, developing the proper disciplines, and determining the drive to succeed, what most people need is a proven road map along with some inspiration to point them in the right direction. We need more details and key points to help lead us to discover our best dreams and then even more help to develop the discipline to reach those dreams and desires that we have *planted* inside of us.

I want to briefly draw your attention back to a specific word that I used in the previous sentence. I consider that word *planted* to be a key word to consider when moving forward. The following word picture will help make the word more understandable.

If you have a dream that is urging you to pursue a certain profession or do something more in life, then that dream is a "seed." That seed was **planted** within you at some point along your life's journey. I firmly believe that the Lord plants His BEST dreams for our lives within us. For those who honor and serve the Lord, those best dreams become the desires of our heart. I also believe that God can use others to reinforce His best dreams and desires planted within us as well. Psalm 37:4 tells us that God grants us the desires of our hearts, and Philippians 2:13 tells us that **God puts those desires in our heart**! If you want to fine-tune your life to His voice, look inside your heart.

Psalm 37:4 NIV
"Take delight in the Lord, and he will give you the desires of your heart."

Philippians 2:13 NIV
"For it is God who works in you to will and to act in order to fulfill his good purpose."

You might have had a dream seed planted in your heart after you finished reading a book in the past about a certain person or a profession that appealed to you. You might have had a dream planted inside of you when you learned about a charitable cause that made you think, *Yes, that really sounds like something I would like to help with.*

Possibly a parent or a teacher helped reinforce a dream seed that inspires you to become a teacher, doctor, lawyer, etc. You may have heard someone speaking at an event or you were listening to an online podcast when something within started resonating, leading you to say, "Yes, I want that for my life one day."

Whatever the case may be, we ALL have our best dreams "planted" within us that must continually be watered, nurtured, and tended for them to grow into what God designed us to be.

However, there is a little more to the story. Discovering your **best** dreams requires some sorting through your thoughts and ideas and distilling them to very specific and defined goals. Reaching the best dreams takes focused and personalized discipline, great intention and drive, as well as goals! Various chapters will dive into and develop each of these valuable elements for success.

I believe the coming chapters will help you sort out your BEST dreams planted inside of you, guide you to develop the disciplines and drive to look beyond your perceived limitations, and help you boldly step into the life you were born to create.

> *"Most great people have attained their greatest success just one step beyond their greatest failure."*
>
> – NAPOLEON HILL

This book is designed to put you on a new path by adapting to a new mindset and a personalized set of disciplines. The intent of each subsequent chapter is to inspire you to go beyond the dreaming stages and embolden you to step into the life you were born to create.

These next thoughts are critical for you to overcome as you move forward. You may already have thoughts and ideas of dreams within you that you want to find the courage to pursue. In fact, many people have already discovered their best dreams inside of them; unfortunately, they spend most of their life only dreaming and never reach deep enough inside to go after them. Instead of embracing their dreams, they practice the same habits, same ideas, and same mindset, never moving forward. Then they wonder why they are not getting any closer to the dreams they have planted inside of them.

Once you understand the correct path to your best life, knowing how to be successful is not a big secret! You must stay focused and be intentional! Be certain you are heading somewhere with a purpose and a passion that burns deep inside of you. You must continually pay attention to the signs as you live life to make certain that the *somewhere* you are headed leads you to the somewhere you are really meant to be.

The very fact that you are reading this book right now shows that you are well ahead of most who will never take the time to pursue their best dreams. Most simply accept the life they have been handed and never do anything more. However, trying and failing is far better than never to try.

So, my friend, I congratulate you on getting this far, but it gets even better the higher up the mountain of life you climb.

"Make certain that the somewhere you are going in life leads you to the somewhere you are really meant to be for your life."

– TOMMY TURNER

"I have not failed; I've just found 10,000 ways that won't work."

– THOMAS A. EDISON

CHAPTER 3
Where Are You Going?

I set the stage in the last chapter to lead into this chapter, so allow me to ask you a question: do you know where you are going in life?

Before you answer, let me share a scenario to bring some additional clarity to this simple question. If someone handed you some random directions to follow for your life, and you decided to take off and follow those directions, then you would eventually end up wherever those directions had led you. That's fine—if those directions are taking you where your life was meant to go.

Please pay very close attention to this next point!

Life will continually try to trip us up and pull us in many different directions, which is exactly why we must discover the BEST dreams for our life. Then we must develop a positive mindset and a personalized set of disciplines to reach the life for which we were designed!

I am certain that many reading this book have been led astray at some point due to bad decisions, difficult circumstances, and much more. But it's never too late to get back on course and follow the life directions that God designed for us! Staying focused and intentional to discover our **best** dreams planted within us is imperative. Then we can follow the path best suited for our life and not nurture the bad seeds meant to keep us from the best life.

Anyone can follow directions that will take them to a place on life's map. However, those directions do little good if those directions lead them to the places that were NOT meant for their life.

Perhaps you made some bad choices in your life that have led to difficult consequences. These challenges have led you to believe that you'll never reach the life you dream of. Additionally, perhaps you have simply been doing your best while trying to find the best path for your life, but you still feel that there must be more. The list of reasons why you may feel like your best life is far away or not possible could be rather long. The good news is that you can make shifts in your mindset and start following the correct directions now.

I would like to offer one more word of encouragement regarding anyone who has made some bad choices in life and/or endured some inconvenient situations. The Lord is fully aware of ALL you have gone through up to this point in your life. He is aware of your bad choices and difficult situations you have faced or will ever go through—even before they exist. The Lord knows every choice—good or bad—you have made or will ever make in life even before you make the decision. He knows every step you have taken on your journey that has led you on the path you are on now.

May I encourage you to seek Him and trust in His ways. He still has amazing plans for your life if you will simply keep pressing on. I am living proof of that promise.

You can change your mindset and begin to realize you were made for something greater. Everyone was created for greatness, and we all come in many different shapes and forms in this life. Your greatness will be completely different from mine and others.

Sadly, I have followed far too many misguided directions in my life, and because of unfortunate past situations, I have made far too many bad choices in my life. I have chased after things that were not the best paths for me to go down, and later, I regretted not being intentional and focused on my best dreams. I am so grateful that God is so merciful and forgiving and never gave up on me. He will never give up on you either if you will put your trust in Him.

Jeremiah 29:11 NKJV
"For I know the thoughts that I think toward
you, says the Lord, thoughts of peace and not
of evil, to give you a future and a hope."

For some, your best dreams may still seem a little distant or unclear right now, but I encourage you to stay the course. I believe by the time you finish this book, they will become noticeably clearer and give you the tools to set you on the right path toward the proper disciplines and mindset to step into the life you were born to create.

For now, let us establish that many vehicles can help get you back on track to discover the successful locations you desire to be in life. You will also meet many challenges and roadblocks along the way. I do not make that point to discourage you, but to give you a reality check.

Most people are simply not willing to put in the long hours, days, weeks, and often years of pressing on to reach their most successful places in life. The fact is, most give up right before they reach a breakthrough to success.

So, why do most people settle or accept their life the way it is and follow whatever directions they are handed in life instead of pressing on to live the life they were born to create?

The next two points are EXTREMLY important in your journey toward living your best dreams. If you are taking notes as you read through this material, I suggest you make a note of these next two points and keep them somewhere easily accessible.

Key Points

- Most people do not recognize or do not believe that they were created for great things by the God of all creation.

Ephesians 2:10 NIV

*"For we are God's handiwork, created in
Christ Jesus to do good works, which God
prepared in advance for us to do."*

- Most people do not recognize that their failures, heartaches, and pain can become some of the best indicators and directions for moving forward toward their BEST dreams.

Romans 8:28 ESV

*"And we know that for those who love God all
things work together for good, for those who
are called according to his purpose."*

This morning as I was doing my Bible reading and devotional study, I found the following entry in my devotional. I found the explanation so fitting for clarifying the thoughts in this chapter.

> *You can achieve the victorious life through living and deep dependence on Me. People usually associate victory with success: not falling or stumbling, not making mistakes. But those who are successful in their own strength tend to go their own way, forgetting about Me. It is through problems and failure, weakness and neediness that you learn to rely on Me.*
>
> *True dependence is not simply asking Me to bless what you have decided to do. It is coming to Me with an open mind and heart, inviting Me to plant My*

desires within you. I may infuse within you a dream that seems far beyond your reach. You know that in yourself you cannot achieve such a goal. Thus begins your journey of profound reliance on Me. It is a faith-walk, taken one step at a time, leaning on Me as much as you need. This is not a path of continual success but of multiple failures. However, each failure is followed by a growth spurt, nourished by increased reliance on Me. Enjoy the blessedness of a victorious life, through deepening your dependence on Me.

2 Corinthians 5:7 NKJV
"For we walk by faith, not by sight."

The words of the Lord are always so refreshing and timely. I trust you will continue to move toward your best dreams planted inside of you. I am hopeful that the thoughts and ideas being presented within these pages will offer you the strength and inspiration to develop proper disciplines and a burning desire to ignite the fire within propelling you toward your goals, dreams, and successes. I encourage you to find a comfortable spot, buckle up, and get ready for the ride of your life. It's about to happen!

As they say at the start of the Daytona 500, "Drivers, start your engines…"

"You must first be who you really are, then do what you need to do, in order to have what you want."
— MARGARET YOUNG

CHAPTER 4
Discovering Your BEST Dreams

When you were a child, you may have had a parent or a grand-parent or another legal guardian who continually instilled thoughts or ideas in your mind pertaining to the dreams they had for your life. Unfortunately, they were without understanding for what you were really created.

Now, quite possibly the Lord has used your parent(s) or others who have influenced your life to help nurture your BEST dreams within for your future successes. Still, if you are uncertain that you are on the right path, perhaps some of those dreams or ideas planted within you are **not** the BEST dream seeds for your life's design.

So, how can you know for sure?

This chapter will challenge some of the dreams or thoughts you've had and will look for signs along the way on your journey of success. A powerful story included in this chapter will help you sort through the various ideas in your mind and help you validate your best dreams.

I have wanted to use the following story in one of my books, and I believe this is the perfect place! The truth I gleaned from this anecdote has helped me test my best dreams in the past.

The Story of a Young Violin Prodigy

A young violin prodigy was walking down the street trying to decide whether to pursue a life in music. As he continued to walk along, he noticed one of the greatest violin teachers in the world standing across the street. He could hardly believe his luck and took it as a sign.

He ran across the street and asked this great teacher if he could play for him. His thought was that if the great teacher did not approve, he would abandon his dream of music and move on to something else. The teacher quietly nodded his head and agreed to listen to the young man play.

The young man began to play his violin. Beads of sweat soon started appearing on his forehead as he played for the teacher. At the end of his piece, he was certain he had just performed one of the greatest performances of his life, but the great teacher simply shook his head and said to the young man, "You lack the fire."

The young man immediately turned and went home dejected. He put away his violin never to pursue his dreams of music again. He later decided to pursue a career in business instead, and as it turned out, he was exceptionally good at it and became remarkably wealthy and successful.

About ten years later, he was walking in another city, when he noticed the expert violin teacher across the street once again. He quickly ran over to him, asking him to stop for a minute.

The teacher stopped, and the man said, "You probably don't remember me, but I played my violin for you several years ago, and you told me that I lacked the fire. Although it was very painful to give up my love of the violin, I want to thank you, as I have become extremely successful in business and for that I am grateful for your wise advice back then."

"However," the young man questioned, "I am curious, how did you know that I lacked what it takes? How did you know that I lacked 'the fire'?"

The great teacher shook his head and said, "You do not understand. I tell everyone who plays for me that they lack 'the fire.' If you had had the fire, you would not have given up so easily."

———

Do you want in on the reality?

Most dreamers <u>lack</u> "the fire." In fact, most of the people who read this book <u>lack</u> "the fire" to achieve their best dreams.

My comments in bold may come as a bit of a surprise since they are being made by me—the author of a book on finding your best dreams and igniting the fire within. However, please hear me out. I promise, good motives are behind my comments, and my motives are slightly different than the wise teacher had for that young violin prodigy. I will expound upon this thought full circle in another chapter.

For now, please set aside any feelings of doubt or questions you might have about my motives for making my "bold" comments for now. I will share my thought process in due time, but first, some more unpacking will set the stage for the positive impact I intend for that statement to make later. Keep pressing on...

So, let me challenge you, as I have challenged myself with the "the fire" question many times in my journey toward my best dreams. Does the dream or thought you are evaluating and considering in your heart give you enough energy, conviction, and fire within to want to set goals and to develop the proper mindset and disciplines to press on—even when things are tough?

I have had many dreams and ideas inside of me over the years, but in the end, I gave up on most of them at the first signs of resistance. I thought I was passionate about a few of them and gave them a real shot, but I was still not willing to sacrifice enough to really press on to achieve those dreams and ideas when difficulties arose.

I simply did not have a fire burning within to fuel most of the thoughts and ideas planted inside of me. In the end, they were only passing thoughts or ideas—not true passions rooted deeply and burning inside of me. However, I NEVER gave up. I kept searching and redefining my goals and dreams.

The BEST dreams planted within you will create a spark that ignites a fire within you to keep pressing on... You must be willing to keep driving and going uphill. If you are willing to work through the objections and drive hard enough to make your dreams happen, then your dream is worth focusing on and working toward.

I have good news! You can overcome any objections to validate a dream—if it is really one of your best dreams! If what you are dreaming for your life is really meant for you and you are willing to develop the proper mindset and disciplines to keep pressing toward it, then you have a very good chance that your dream is one of your best dreams planted within you.

If you feel a fire beginning to ignite within you, then you are doing well. If you are still not sure, then ask yourself this question: do you want to keep pressing on to find your BEST dreams?

> *"Never let the fear of striking out keep you from playing the game."*

> — BABE RUTH

I am confident that you will discover many more valuable suggestions in the pages ahead!

CHAPTER 5
What if MONEY Did Not Matter?

There are several reasons why someone will not develop the proper mindset and discipline to chase after a dream, but MONEY is often one of the main excuses most give for not pursuing a dream. Though the lack of confidence is often the second reason, in this chapter I want to address the money excuse.

You may assume that most struggle due to the *lack* of money. However, I have found there are two sides to the money question. Yes, often the lack of money keeps a person from pursuing a dream, but stepping away from a comfortable income to chase after a dream is also a consideration for some. A person with a good paying job cannot imagine leaving behind that security—even when deep inside that person wants to be somewhere other than where he is currently in life.

What would you think if I said that money is the least of a person's worries when it comes to going after your BEST dreams?

I believe you might ask, "Who will pay my bills if I step away from a good paying job? Who will fund my dreams when I have no money?"

Remember the prodigy who gave up on becoming a violin virtuosi? If you had *the fire* he did not have, then you would not give up so easily. If you really want that dream, you will find the drive to press on toward your **best** dreams. However, if you lack *the fire,* then you will likely give up and quit.

Securing a dream is never really about money. Rather, pursuing a dream is always about discovering your **best** dreams, igniting the fire within, and pressing on to reach them!

> *"Your BEST dreams and excuses should mix like oil and water!"*
>
> – TOMMY TURNER

Several years ago, I was meeting with a life coach at her office to evaluate and establish some direction in my life. During this session with the life coach, she handed me a "magic wand" and told me to wave it to create my ideal life and then describe to her what I saw.

That visual really did not work well for me at the time. Maybe it seemed too simple or make-believe for me, I guess. At the time I felt the problem limiting me personally involved a myriad of reasons, including the lack of money, ability, grit, and confidence.

So, I joked, "How could a magic wand help?" Plus, the more I thought about her visual aid, I realized I did not even believe in the concept of a magic wand in the first place! However, the real problem was not the magic wand concept at all. The issue was that I simply had the wrong mindset! I had too many excuses and not enough intention and drive to discover my best dreams.

I used to continually ask myself the question: "What if money did not matter?" Blaming my ineffectiveness on a lack of funds was so easy!

The same is true for you, and stepping away from a good paying job, even when you are unhappy in that job, is even harder.

However, I will still hammer home the fact that if you want something bad enough, then not even the lack of money or the comfort of money can stop you.

If you REALLY want to achieve that goal, you will find the means to fund it or be willing to sacrifice the comforts of a good paying job while you press on to make your best dreams come true.

> *"If you're serious about changing your life, you'll find a way. If you're not, you'll find an excuse."*
>
> — JEN SINCERO

I have shared numerous times in all my books that I am a man of faith. I have learned to trust daily in the Lord's direction for my life. I mention my faith for those who have faith in the Lord as well. I realize that not everyone will believe as I do, and I totally respect that choice. However, I strongly encourage and implore those believers who feel a burning desire within to go after a dream to have the faith to chase after their best dreams.

However, regardless of our beliefs, we ALL have dreams and desires planted within us. If what you discover is truly one of your best dreams, then you will find a way to ignite the fire and develop the proper mindset and disciplines to bring that dream to fruition—even if it takes you several years.

If you do not mind, I would like to say a quick prayer for those who would be open to seeking that best dream.

> *Lord, as we progress through this book, I pray for those who are still trying to figure out what dreams inside are their best dreams and desires planted by You. Lord, I ask that Your Holy Spirit guide them to discover the desires of their heart and ignite a fire within them to chase after their BEST dreams. Amen.*

We all have our best dreams planted inside of us and as we accomplish some of our best dreams and goals, the best dreams often get even bigger, as they have in my case. Keep climbing higher up the mountain of life; the view is fantastic!

The following quote by Mark Twain is one of my favorites pertaining to life and dreams!

> *"The two most important days in your life are **the day you are born and the day you find out why."***
>
> – MARK TWAIN

Ask Yourself These Two Questions

- What am I good at?
- What am I passionate about?

If you can answer these two questions with confidence, then you will develop the discipline to ignite the fire to keep driving…

If you are still not there yet, keep pressing on anyway until you find the direction you are supposed to be headed. Be certain you are not driving around in a circle! In the following pages, we will continue to work toward moving forward in a positive direction.

> *"A tree does not stop growing because the wind blew off a few of its leaves."*
>
> – MATSHONA DHLIWAYO

CHAPTER 6
The Search for Happiness

I am always so amazed by the talents and gifts of others who are living their best dreams. I was so inspired by a popular motivational story circulated on social media in 2020. I feel this story which dealt with happiness will help add some value and clarity to your life as well as you search for your best dreams.

The Story of the Balloon

A wise teacher once brought some balloons into her classroom. She instructed the students to blow up a balloon and then write their name on the balloon. The entire class did this exercise.

Then all the students threw their balloons into the school hallway. The teacher walked through the balloons in the hallway tossing them around and mixing them all up. "Class, you have five minutes to find the balloon with your name on it."

The children frantically searched, but not one student was able to find the balloon with his or her name written on it.

"Class," she said, "pick up the balloon nearest to you and take it to the person whose name is written on it."

Within two minutes every student was holding the balloon with his or her name on it.

"Class," the teacher said, "this is the secret to finding happiness. Searching for your own happiness can be difficult. But when you help others find their happiness, then you will also find happiness."

———

I believe this story brings some valuable perspective for evaluating the purpose of your dreams. Hopefully, you will find clarity when searching for the BEST dreams planted inside of you.

Many people are chasing after their dreams, searching everywhere to find happiness and create a better life for themselves. However, they often miss the most valuable aspects of life. Please don't misunderstand me. Nothing is wrong with wanting to live a good life filled with success and happiness. In fact, that goal is a great one to pursue, and I trust this book will help inspire you to keep driving toward the life you desire.

However, if you understand and apply the lesson given in this online story of helping others find their happiness, you will find your happiness much sooner! The goal should always be to serve others and add value to them. This key aspect to living a disciplined, successful, and happy life is so simple, yet very profound.

Zig Ziglar, the great motivational speaker, said it very appropriately in the following quote.

> *"You can have everything in life you want if you will just help other people get what they want."*
>
> — ZIG ZIGLAR

I would like to conclude this chapter by sharing a personal experience that really brought the point of this chapter to life for me. Those who associate with me know that I am a big college sports fan! Since my hometown is Eugene, Oregon, I root for the Oregon Ducks, one of my favorite college teams. In fact, even as I work on this chapter, I'm excitedly planning to attend an Oregon women's basketball game tonight.

Even if you don't happen to be an Oregon Duck fan, please stay with me anyway. The reason I mention this personal fact is because one of the assistant coaches for the Oregon Duck men's basketball team is a piano-tuning customer of mine.

Recently when I was at his home tuning their piano, the Ducks had lost a tough game the night before to a team they really should have defeated. Understandably, the coach was bummed over the loss but, like always, he was handling the loss with real class. He was already studying for the next game, determined the team will get back at it the next week.

After I had finished tuning his piano, I gave him a copy of my book *Quick Charge Your Life*. We talked for a bit about life and Oregon basketball. I offered him some words of encouragement and how much I appreciated his drive and passion for the game and the young men over whom he had influence. I could tell he really appreciated my words at that moment.

Being a HUGE Oregon Duck fan like I am, you have no idea what a *"Quick-Charge"* thrill moment that was for me to talk ball with one of the assistant coaches for a top-rated college team! Not many of us diehard "everyday" fans get the privilege of talking shop with a top-notch coach.

After our brief conversation concluded, I asked him to also pass along another copy of *Quick Charge Your Life* to the head coach, Dana Altman. As I am writing this illustration, I have no idea if he ever passed on the book to Dana, but that is not the point. What I find amazing is that I lived my dream that day by adding value to someone else, and in turn, I received so much value and happiness! This assistant coach has a huge influence over young men, and some of those young men will go on to play in the NBA and have influence over many others as well.

You never know, but perhaps something I shared that day with the assistant coach may inspire him to press on to more successes. He may also pass along some inspiring thoughts that he discovers through reading one of my books, and those inspiring thoughts may continue forward and inspire some of those young men on the basketball team over whom he has some influence.

Maybe some of those young men will share the messages forward as well and impact people I may never even meet here on earth. Wow! The opportunity to add value to someone else's life is so energizing and amazing.

Learn it, live it, and inspire others...
Quick Charge Your Life!

As I conclude this chapter, I would like to share one more quick point about this assistant basketball coach that I feel is valuable. This coach is clearly living his BEST dreams and serving in his zone of giftedness. Anyone who knows him or watches him interact with his team during a game or in practice would tell you that he is passionate about what he does. I have a feeling that he would do his job for free if the bills were paid. He may also have even bigger dreams of being a head coach of a major college team one day himself. I guess time will tell.

If you are still searching for your best dreams inside of you, then I encourage you to look for opportunities to add value to people and serve others. Your best dreams will find a way of surfacing as you keep serving and adding value to others.

> *"The whole secret of a successful life is to find out what is one's destiny to do, and then do it."*
>
> – HENRY FORD

CHAPTER 7
More Than One Dream

As you continue sorting through your ideas and thoughts in search of your best dreams, allow me to share some insight about my own life's journey to discovering my best dreams that will help you understand what you might be seeking.

The first point that I want to stress as you search for your best dreams is that you may be looking for more than one dream or passion. You may have noticed that I often use the plural form of the word "dream" instead of the singular form.

I am certain that had I been more focused and disciplined at a younger age I would not have travelled the rough and rocky road that I have had to travel. Thankfully, my desire to keep pressing on to reach my promised land and to live the life I was born to create has paid dividends in my life many times over.

I still have many more goals to achieve on my journey to reach my BIGGEST dreams, but I have come a remarkable distance since the early stages of my life's journey. I have already mentioned that in addition to being an author, I am also in the piano business.

I have had a love for pianos and how they function and sound for more than 40 years at this writing. However, when I was younger, I never really "dreamed" of being in the piano business. When I was in my mid-twenties, I saw a row of grand pianos all shining in the lights of a piano store one night. A flame began to light up within me, and at that very moment, I had an overwhelming feeling that I would really love to work with pianos. At that time, I was working with my dad in our family business, enjoying the benefits of a good paying career.

That night I mustered up the courage to tell my dad that I really wanted to leave the business and apply for a job at that piano store. Thinking he might not approve since we were basically a two-man operation, I quickly discovered that he was thrilled I had a passion for piano.

Knowing I had an interest in that field, he encouraged me to apply for a sales job at the piano store. The very next day, I did as he advised and applied. Unbelievably, my timing could not have been more perfect. When I walked into the piano store to apply, a man wearing a big black cowboy hat passed by me on his way out the door. That man had just given his two-week notice, so an opening had indeed come available, and I was hired on the spot.

I hit the ground running with this new career. As it turned out, I was pretty good at selling the pianos, but watching the piano tuner come in and work on pianos every week started to light an even bigger fire inside of me.

Unfortunately, the owner of that piano store had financial issues so that piano sales job ended rather quickly, but the valuable experience I received while working in this piano store lit a new flame within. After this piano store closed, my wife at the time and I moved back to the Eugene area.

As it turned out, after I moved back to the Eugene area, I began working at a large clothing store **across the street from another piano store**! My love of pianos was still very much alive, and my *"fire"* to pursue a career in the piano industry was still burning strong. I was desperately searching for any way possible to get back into the piano business as soon as I could find an opening. Now, let me set the stage for the events that followed.

I happened to have some rather interesting history with Wayne Wagner, the store manager of this piano store across the street. I had purchased a new Baldwin piano from this store a few years earlier. Wayne remembered me very well because they had delivered two different pianos to my home on two separate occasions, but I was not happy with either one of them after taking delivery.

Wayne finally told me that I had one last opportunity to come back into the store and pick out another piano, and that third piano was the final one I could have delivered. This time I found the perfect piano, but little did I know at the time that encounter would later become the beginning of a lifelong career.

After starting my new job across the street from this piano store, I would run across the street on my lunch breaks to play the pianos and beg Wayne for a job. He would always say, "We are a family-owned business, but I appreciate your drive and desire to work in the piano business."

I had gotten married less than a year before moving back to the Eugene area and taking this job at the clothing store when I wanted to be at the piano store. Knowing that I had married shortly before accepting this job across from this piano store sets the stage for the second leg of this story.

After a couple of months had passed, I was still begging Wayne for a job. One evening I was visiting with my wife's brothers and their wives. I believe one of her family members asked me what I planned to do for a living. I told them that I loved pianos and would really like to get a job working at another piano store one day. I then mentioned that I was working across the street from a piano store in Eugene, and I enjoyed visiting the manager on my lunch break. I then mentioned that I continually begged the store manager, Wayne Wagner, for a job.

At that very moment, my new sister-in-law Cherilynn said, "You do know that Wayne Wagner is my dad, right?" I could hardly believe what she said. I guess I had never paid much attention to what her maiden name had been or the correlation. So, the very next day I marched over to the piano store and explained to Wayne that I was *family*.

We both chuckled at the crazy coincidence as he had no idea about our connection either. However, that commonality opened the doors to a new conversation that carried on for a few more weeks. Then one day, Wayne handed me some books on piano tuning and repair and suggested that I consider becoming a piano tuner. "Then I can hire you to work in the store." To make a long story short, I heeded his advice, and piano tuning has turned into an amazing, lifelong career for me.

Now, to make my point: yes, I do love tuning pianos and working in the piano business. This business is truly one of the BEST dreams of my life, but I still had other dreams planted inside of me yet to be discovered.

I have always loved the stock market. Many years ago, I had a dream of also becoming a stockbroker or a financial advisor. I started buying and selling stocks through a stockbroker in the early '80s, and my interest in stocks and investing in the financial markets continued to expand over the years.

The thought was that I could still tune pianos in the evenings and on weekends but become a full-time financial advisor or stockbroker during the day. The idea of managing millions of dollars as a financial planner and helping people to build wealth to live a more comfortable life or enjoy a better retirement sounded so exciting and fulfilling to me.

However, I can now testify that after pursuing that career idea, I did not have a fire burning inside of me to risk it all to work full-time in the financial industry, per se, but I did have enough drive to test the idea. I even went as far as to get a job working for the Edward Jones Financial Services around 2007-2008. I soon discovered the market conditions were less than favorable at the time, and I simply did not have the fire within that I thought I had. I gave up on this dream at the first signs of difficulty.

However, I still receive immense joy and satisfaction from trading and investing in stocks daily. Although I do really enjoy trading stocks, I had to readjust my ideals of what I had originally thought was one of my "best dreams" of becoming a financial advisor or a stockbroker and discovered that one of my best dreams was to trade and invest in my own stock portfolio and not manage money for others.

Then, several years later, I also discovered that I had an interest in writing. However, I did not discover my love for writing until much later in life when I was well into my late 50s. Now writing books and inspiring others is another strong passion of mine that lights a burning fire deep within. However, this dream started as a flickering flame that progressed into a roaring fire over time. I still LOVE to tune and service pianos, and I still LOVE trading stocks daily, but I have diversified my interests and discovered that I have multiple BEST dreams in my life.

I share all of these best dreams to make this point: you may very well have multiple interests that also light a flame. However, that nice flame does not burst into a consuming fire that makes you willing to step out and pursue your dream full time. Still, that lack of fire does not mean that you simply leave behind those interests.

No two people are alike in this entire world. You may have multiple fires burning inside or flames that will turn into a fire over time. Perhaps, like me, you will find a way to combine your best dreams together and pursue more than one of your passions at the same time. When it comes to chasing your best dreams, there are NO RULES.

If you have multiple interests like me, and you're trying to sort out which one to pursue, then you may not be seeking only one dream. I realize that I am wired differently than many. I have a passion to keep pressing on and pursuing *all* my dreams. I will rest when I get to heaven, but for now, I plan to keep chasing ALL my best dreams and continue to live the life I have been created for.

In closing, we have a saying in the piano business that a piano chooses a person just as much as the person chooses a piano. Well, I believe the same is true with your best dreams. Your best dreams are searching for you as much as you are searching for them! Don't ever give up!

Your best dreams will find you, and you will find them at the right time. The place you finally meet each other is magical. Keep dreaming, keep pressing on, and keep exploring all your interests until a fire begins to rage inside.

> *"Dream as if you'll live forever.*
> *Live as if you'll die today."*
>
> – JAMES DEAN

CHAPTER 8
You Lack the Fire

The time has come to circle back to the comment I made in chapter four: **most dreamers <u>lack</u> "the fire."** In fact, **most of the people who read this book <u>lack</u> "the fire" to achieve their best dreams.**

I explained that I had a motive for my comments, and that my motives were slightly different than the wise teacher's testing the young violin prodigy. In that story, the young violin prodigy gave up on his dreams of pursuing a career in music because the great teacher told him he lacked "the fire." That young man then became a successful businessman. He later credited the wise teacher for giving him such good and knowledgeable advice by telling him he lacked "the fire."

However, the great teacher had not given this young violinist any profound or personal advice at all. As the teacher explained to the young man many years later, he told every potential violinist who played for him that they lacked "the fire."

Are you wondering about my motives for making these comments?

1) **I am not you.** In all likelihood I do not know you personally, and even if I did know you personally, I am not you. So, what I think or say about your best dreams and drive for success should not be taken personally. You should not allow my words to knock you off course. Neither should you take personally or allow what others think or say about your best dreams and drive for success knock you off course. What the WORLD thinks or says about your best dreams and drive for success should not be taken personally and knock you off course. All that should matter to you is what the Lord's opinion is of you and your best dreams. He created you and knew what you are capable of accomplishing.

    I have good news…*the Lord is highly in favor of you and your abilities to live the life you were born to create!*

    From the moment you were conceived, the Lord had a plan for your life. He already knew the circumstances you would encounter and the mistakes you would make in life. He already knew what your name would be. He already knew you would be reading this sentence at this very exact moment in time.

    You only need to win one battle, and that battle is the one that goes on inside your head. If you believe in your best dreams, then it should not matter if I or anyone else feels you lack "the fire."

2) **Make a very small adjustment by changing one <u>word</u> to give this statement a totally different message.** What if you removed the word *lack* and inserted the word *have*? **Most dreamers *have* "the fire."** Most of the people who read this book also *have* "the fire" to achieve their best dreams. The fact is both statements could be 100 percent true. One is as valid as the other. My friend, you do *have* "the fire" within to discover and live your best dreams!

    Whether or not someone is for you or against you should not be taken personally and knock you off course. The bottom line is being willing to make a small mindset change to tap into the knowledge and understanding that the Lord has an amazing plan for your life. He knows who you are and what He is working with, so you must simply let Him guide you to the life you were born to create.

If I knew you personally, I could believe with all my might that you will succeed and accomplish your best dreams. I could support you, cheer for you, and give you all the great advice in the world, but in the end, what I could do for you would not ensure your success. Your personal success ultimately comes down to what the Lord says and your ability to press on, believing in Him and His promises for your life.

Jeremiah 29:11 NIV
"For I know the plans I have for you," declares
the Lord, "plans to prosper you and not to harm
you, plans to give you hope and a future."

To get to the best places the Lord has planned for you will take discipline and drive. Even if you do not believe in the Lord, His plans for your life do not change. He created you for a purpose regardless of whether or not you accept Him.

As you continue to read this book, you do not need to be a rocket scientist or a detective like Sherlock Holmes to discover that my life is far from perfect. I can point to many times in my past when I was living my life in disobedience without the Lord.

I have faced many obstacles that have come and gone in my life. If I were a judge and had to assess my own life, I might rule myself as undeserving and not worthy of His forgiveness, grace, mercy, and the bountiful successes I enjoy today. Thankfully, I am not the judge—nor is anyone else—so don't let anyone stop you! But even more importantly, don't stop yourself. If you know you have your best dreams in sight, then go after them.

Currently, I am living one of my best dreams and writing a book to encourage you to live your best dreams. Even while I am living my best dream, I cannot say that my life is perfect by any means. Much in my life has slowed my progress to success due to bad choices, unfortunate circumstances, and even more, but the Lord still has a plan for my life. Rest assured; He has a plan for your life as well.

I am driven, disciplined, and living my best life now, but I have many more goals and best dreams that I still want to achieve as well.

I feel every person should always be growing and learning, never settling for where he or she is in life. I am not saying we shouldn't appreciate and enjoy our life and successes every day. However, life is a journey, and none of us know the day and or time when our life will come to an end. Therefore, we must always be striving to discover and live out our best dreams every single day we are breathing on this earth.

> *"Your words control your life, your progress, your results, even your mental and physical health. You cannot talk like a failure and expect to be successful."*
> – GERMANY KENT

CHAPTER 9
How Are You Wired?

Everyone has attributes that make him or her uniquely different from others outside of the obvious such as gender, race, and other physical characteristics. We all have certain quirks, habits, and personalities that make us the unique individuals that we are.

For instance, some people have an issue with the number 13 and consider it unlucky, whereas others regard the number 13 as their lucky number. Others, of course, could care less. In fact, some hotels in Vegas do not have a thirteenth floor as some guests would not stay there because of their superstitions.

Obviously, people are unique and different in many ways. Some people need to spend several hours alone each day to recharge, read, think, and rest. Others can only enjoy life and recharge when surrounded by people almost constantly.

What is unique about discovering your best dreams and living the life you were born to create is because God only made *one* YOU! Every person ever born is wired and designed differently—not one other person is exactly like you in the entire world. If you could literally meet and talk with every single person who has ever walked the face of this earth, you would not find another YOU. Possibly, you would find a few people who looked almost exactly like you, but they would still be slightly different in some way or another.

You might meet several people who enjoy the same interests and hobbies, and whose habits mirror yours, but you would still find some differences. You might even meet someone who is not the same gender as you, but you would swear they are the opposite-gender version of YOU.

However, of all the billions of people in this world, you will NOT find anyone wired and designed exactly like YOU. I mention this fact to inspire you to continue pressing on to discover your best dreams and step into the life YOU were born to create. The world is waiting for YOU to be the YOU that God created YOU to be!

> *"You were born an original; don't die a copy."*
> – JOHN MASON

I wrote this chapter as a late addition to the book, but the truth I have presented is so important to grasp. I cannot believe that I thought I was almost done with the main body of this book's content and was already working on the conclusion when the thought of using helpful tools to learn more about how we are wired came to me. Thus, another chapter developed.

I found taking a personality test helpful when searching for my best dreams and the best version of myself. Taking various online and written tests can help a person understand how he or she is wired. Many good tests are available online or in written form. Some online tests will be free, whereas others will have a small fee attached to them. I am not suggesting that you take multiple personality tests and whatever else exists to discover what your strengths are; however, I do suggest checking out a few different tests to see what type of results you get.

The purpose of this chapter is not to promote any certain personality or career test. However, I do suggest that you do a Google search for **personality test and/or career test**. I have probably taken a dozen paid and free tests over the years, both written and online tests. I personally found them extremely helpful to narrow down my interests and best dreams.

I also suggest taking a few different online as well as written tests and then comparing all the results to see the commonalities. I found slight differences in my own results, but I also saw some very common trends that helped me to understand how I am wired. I trust this suggestion will help you to gain some clarity as well.

> *"The world is waiting for YOU to be the YOU that God created YOU to be"*
>
> – TOMMY TURNER

> *"Success is personal, so stop comparing your apples to their oranges"*
>
> – YOHANCÉ SALIMU

SECTION TWO

Define Your Goals

CHAPTER 10
Keeping It All in Perspective

Before engaging in the process of defining goals, having a little perspective on life is also important. I believe human nature wants to be comfortable, happy, successful, and fulfilled, but what do those intangibles really look like? There are many ideas as to what success, happiness, and fulfillment look like for each person.

For one person, happiness and success would be to own a home in the country with lots of acreage. Having a large following online and being an influencer through social media would mean happiness and success to another. For another, happiness and success would be defined as staying at home to be a mother and raise a happy family. Running a Fortune 500 company would mean happiness and success for yet another.

Many people often associate being happy and successful with having more money, a nicer house, a newer car, name-brand clothing, popularity, more time, freedom, a better job, and so forth. Yes, being able to have all those would be great, but I want to add some perspectives to life.

Over the many years I have studied success and happiness, I cannot help but think back to those who have come before us. I am reminded of people who were considered wealthy in the 1800s and the early 1900s who had so little in the way of comfort, conveniences, and opportunities compared to a large majority of Americans living today.

I am not suggesting many Americans are wealthier in the sense of having ample funds in the bank and living the high life. Rather, I am suggesting that many Americans are wealthy based on the conveniences and opportunities they enjoy today—not to mention that many have the means to generate incredible incomes today.

The person with enough drive can build an online following and make millions on YouTube, Instagram, and other social media platforms. Our world today with its endless opportunities and bountiful conveniences is very different from the one in which people lived not that long ago.

I can still recall life back in the 70s and 80s before iPhones, YouTube, Google, Amazon, and so many other advancements and companies on which we rely so heavily today. Just imagine a world without Siri, Google, Netflix, YouTube, and Amazon... Not all that long ago many lived in a much simpler world without all the opportunities and conveniences we enjoy today. Imagine life even earlier in the 1700s, 1800s, and into the early 1900s before most Americans even enjoyed simple everyday conveniences such as comfortable cars, television, indoor plumbing, phones, and so forth.

John Davison Rockefeller Sr. (1839-1937) was an American business magnate and philanthropist. According to Wikipedia, he has been widely considered the wealthiest American of all time and the richest person in modern history. Rockefeller was born into a large family in upstate New York and moved several times before eventually settling in Cleveland.

During his lifetime, the senior Rockefeller never had anything remotely close to the conveniences, luxuries, and opportunities that many Americans enjoy today. He might have had tremendous financial wealth, yet he still could not live or purchase the incredible lifestyles many average Americans enjoy today.

We have nicer homes, better cars, better health care, endless opportunities to generate wealth, and more conveniences than I can possibly list on the pages of this book! Yes, even with all his financial wealth, Mr. Rockefeller Sr. could not have possibly dreamed of all the incredible "wealth" that the average American enjoys today...that we consider a normal everyday lifestyle.

So, let me ask you: what is it that you are really going after or searching for in life?

I feel certain that my book is probably not the first one you have read on discovering your best dreams, defining your goals, developing your discipline, and determining your drive to chase after your best dreams and reach success. More than likely, mine won't be your last.

I am not suggesting that anyone who is reading this book is complaining about everything in life or is desperately searching for riches, fame, luxury, and possessions. In fact, I doubt that most are looking for that as their ultimate dream and drive to succeed. But to keep things in perspective, never forget that most of us alive today enjoy many more conveniences, opportunities, and comforts than the wealthiest people from centuries before us.

The key word I am addressing is **opportunities**! The boundless opportunities available to us today to change our mindsets, achieve our goals, and live out our best dreams are endless. We simply need to have the proper perspectives, tools, mindset, and DRIVE to get there!

> *"When one door closes, another door opens, but we so often look so long and so regretfully upon the closed door, that we do not see the ones which open for us."*
>
> — ALEXANDER GRAHAM BELL

CHAPTER 11
Setting Proper Goals

Defining a goal helps bring your dreams into better focus, but goals are only targets—not the prize. Some people will set many goals but never achieve much. Others will set goals that will be too easily reached, only reach a few, and still not get very far in living their best life. Others will set extremely high goals to really push themselves, yet they lack the discipline and fire within to reach most of those lofty goals.

The tricky thing about goals is that they are easy to set and can give you a false sense of accomplishment. I believe the reason that setting goals is tricky is because setting a goal is no major accomplishment. Because people often give themselves too much credit for setting a goal, I want to first establish that setting goals is not all that difficult. Reaching them and moving on to the next goal, then the following goal, and so on really separates the haves from the have nots. Yes, my friend, consistently reaching your goals is where the rubber meets the road and tests your best dreams!

However, one very important aspect to setting goals is first determining some target "goals" in order to hit anything.

For a goal to work, it must have the following five key elements!
+ The goal must be specific.
+ The goal must be measurable.
+ The goal must have a time limit.
+ The goal must be visible in writing.
+ The goal must be challenging.

For starters, consider adopting the following seven-week goal challenge. Write down three activities you would like to incorporate in your daily routine over the next seven weeks. Then ask yourself which of those three activities means the most to you. Perhaps I should say it this way: which of the three activities you chose is the most challenging for you to start? Determine that you will NOT fail to accomplish your top goal but challenge yourself to complete all three goals.

The following are some examples of good starting goals you might want to choose or adapt:
+ Walk one mile three times a week for seven weeks.
+ Go to the gym for thirty minutes three times a week for seven weeks.
+ Do thirty pushups and thirty sit-ups four days a week for seven weeks.
+ Read a non-fiction book at least thirty minutes three times a week for seven weeks.
+ Research a favorite subject online for thirty minutes four times a week for seven weeks.
+ Study a foreign language for fifteen minutes three times a week for seven weeks.
+ Purpose to speak three positive affirmations to yourself every morning for seven weeks.

- Read three inspirational quotes per day four times a week for seven weeks.
- Watch two inspirational videos on YouTube at least three times a week for seven weeks.
- Journal your life's journey at least four times a week in a journal for seven weeks.

As you are accomplishing the goals you choose, you will develop more goals as your best dreams come into better focus. If a goal seems like an abundance of work or you lack the desire to really stay focused and press through to accomplish a goal, then the goal is not the issue. Rather, you still lack the fire.

When you have a strong desire and fire burning within you to reach a dream, the goals are only targets to hit along the way. As you develop the proper disciplines and mindset, you can start setting and hitting your target "goals" as you gain momentum and focus on your best dreams.

Set Your Goals in Seven Areas in Life

Now that you understand the five keys behind setting goals, it's time to think about the seven types of goals you need to set.

1. Spiritual Goals

Spiritual goals, the most important category, sets the stage for the others and will help keep you focused on God.

Some Goal-setting Ideas
- In the next thirty days, set a goal to pray ten minutes each day for forty days.
- In the next week start reading one chapter in your Bible three days a week for seven weeks.

- In the next sixty days, challenge yourself to start attending church at least three times a month for three months.

2. Financial Goals

Goals involving money are some of the most difficult to set. However, determining a few simple financial goals can set your finances in order.

Some Goal-setting Ideas
- Create a budget in the next four weeks.
- Pay off a burdensome credit card bill in the next six months.
- Set a goal in the next sixty days to start setting aside at least 3 percent of your paycheck and continue every month for six months.

3. Career Goals

If you are doing work that does not bring you fulfillment, then you need to set a goal to change careers. No one should ever force himself to work in an environment that does not enhance his or her God-given talent.

Some Goal-setting Ideas
- Register for night classes online in the next three months, and for six months, study a subject you are passionate about.
- Over the next thirty days, clearly define at least one area in which you are good and about which you feel passionate.
- Set a goal in the next two weeks to spend thirty minutes per day searching for ideas online to ignite a passion and continue for the next three months.

- Challenge yourself over the next three weeks to talk to at least three friends or family members and ask them what they feel you are good at.

4. Intellectual Goals

You are never too old to learn. I am always studying, taking notes, and learning every day—a wonderful practice I highly recommend and plan to do for the rest of my life.

Some Goal-setting Ideas
- Start reading good non-fiction books in the next sixty days for thirty minutes a day and continue every day for thirty minutes a day for the next eight weeks.
- Set a goal to stop using social media in the next thirty days and then stay away from social media for thirty days.
- Set a goal to turn off the television in the next thirty days and spend time challenging yourself by practicing a new skill for one hour per night for sixty days.

5. Fitness Goals

Developing a good physical routine that benefits your body physically is essential to success.

Some Goal-setting Ideas
- Find time to relax and rest at least one hour every day for the next ninety days.
- In the next thirty days, develop at least one exercise routine (sit-ups, exercise bike, rowing machine, walking, jogging, etc.) for five minutes per day and continue for ninety days.
- Set up a diet plan in the next thirty days to eat less processed food and more fresh food and follow it every day for ninety days.

6. Family Goals

Spending time with those you love is so important to your success. This time should be well spent and not "just because." Spending time with family should be uplifting and joyful.

Some Goal-setting Ideas
- Contact a friend in the next thirty days and invite him or her over or go out for coffee or simply to visit at least once every two weeks and continue for three months.
- Take your spouse or significant other on a date night in the next thirty days and continue once per week for three months.
- Tell someone close to you how much you appreciate him or her in the next two weeks and continue at least once per day for eight weeks.

7. Social Goals

Now this goal will likely provoke a few people, but spending hours on Facebook or other social media sites does not count! So many people today isolate themselves and spend far too much time online interacting through a social media site rather than making the effort to connect with one another in person.

I do believe there is certainly a place for social media activities. I do enjoy checking on Facebook friends or reading a twitter post or two and even looking at cool posts on Instagram. However, when social media becomes all-consuming, you must be disciplined to break that habit.

Some Goal-setting Ideas
- Get involved in a small group or activity at your local church in the next ninety days and continue for six months.

- Find a local charity in the next ninety days and volunteer once a week and continue for three months.
- Organize a get-together with friends and family for a social group in the next sixty days and continue once a month for six months.

> *"If you're bored with life—you don't get up every morning with a burning desire to do things—you don't have enough goals."*
>
> — LOU HOLTZ

You have likely noticed that I set specific time frames to start and stop on these sample goal suggestions. The idea is to see which of your goals begins to ignite a fire within, propelling you closer to your dreams. As you find goals that ignite a fire and add value to others, then you can set new goals that will carry on even longer. Eventually, you can make them bigger and more challenging.

The following insert from my recent journal reading is very appropriate for this section on setting goals.

I AM WITH YOU AND FOR YOU. When you decide on a course of action that is in line with My will, nothing in heaven or on earth can stop you. You may encounter many obstacles as you move toward your goal, but don't be discouraged—never give up! With My help, you can overcome any obstacle. Do not expect an easy path as you journey hand in hand with Me, but do remember that I, your very-present Helper, am omnipotent.

Much, much stress results from your wanting to make things happen before their times have come.

One of the main ways I assert My sovereignty is in the timing of events. If you want to stay close to Me and do things My way, ask Me to show you the path forward moment by moment. Instead of dashing headlong toward your goal, let Me set the pace. Slow down and enjoy the journey in My presence.

Romans 8:31
What, then, shall we say in response to these things? If God is for us, who can be against us?

"*Successful people do things that the average person is not willing to do. They make sacrifices the average person is not willing to make. But the difference it makes is extraordinary.*"

– BRIAN TRACY

"*If you go to work on your goals, your goals will go to work on you. If you go to work on your plan, your plan will go to work on you. Whatever good things we build end up building us.*"

– JIM ROHN

CHAPTER 12
What's Your Timeline?

In 2022 I decided to revisit my life memories and recreate a timeline of key moments in my life thus far. I started with those that I felt impacted me the most over the past 40 years or so. Then I charted my life from that point on to the present. I have faced many struggles and catastrophic failures, as well as enjoying accomplishments and successes along the way.

As you read through my timeline, I am almost certain that you will be shocked and amazed by the levels of success I have enjoyed in spite of all the mistakes and challenges I have experienced. One of the purposes for revealing my timeline is to show if I can be successful and live my best dreams, then I am fully convinced that anyone can!

Over the next three to five weeks, I encourage you to set a goal to write out your own timeline history to see where you have been and where you are going. Then I encourage you to continue keeping track of your timeline, noting your failures, struggles, accomplishments, and successes as they come and go throughout your years moving forward.

I do not consider this project like a journal, but rather recording a short highlight of your progress and/or setbacks for each year. You will only record events that you feel are good or bad highlights throughout each year.

To stay focused on your goals and best dreams means charting both your successes and failures. Your entries should be relatively brief but with enough detail to recall all your thoughts and memories on the various events in your life. After completing this project, you may be surprised at how motivated and focused you will become to chase after your dreams after seeing the highlights—both good and bad—of your life's timeline journey thus far.

I want to share a peek into my past and some perspectives on my journey to success and living my best dreams as a possible guide for you.

Tommy's Timeline

1960-1980 — Far too much life for me to recall the many details that carried me into young adulthood.

1981-1983 — After dropping out of college, I worked for a modeling agency in Seattle. I briefly fell into an unhealthy lifestyle of partying and living wildly. I left the modeling world, moved home to Springfield, Oregon, where I met and married a beautiful girl, then found myself divorced within a very short time interval. My adult life was not off to a very good start.

1983-1985 — I became interested in the stock market and began buying and selling stocks through a local stockbroker, but I made unwise decisions at the time. I also met another amazing woman and married again.

1985-1987 — I left the business my dad and I had started, accepting a temporary job at a piano store selling pianos in Bellevue, Washington. After losing that job through no fault of my own, I returned to Eugene, Oregon, and began working at a clothing store across the street from a familiar piano store. I am reintroduced to Wayne Wagner, who spurs my interest in piano tuning. I went to school in Texas and became a certified piano technician. I had an allergic reaction while at school in Texas that nearly took my life.

1987-1990 — These years begin some bright spots in my life! In January 1987 I graduated from college in Texas, and one month later, I started my piano service career. Then came the birth of my two amazing children, Kristina in October 1987, and Andrew in October 1989. I tuned a piano for Johnny Cash and his wife, June Carter Cash, for a local fair concert—the thrill of a lifetime that led to more encounters with the Cashes and many other famous stars in the music industry. I met Arnold Palmer, Jack Nicklaus, Payne Stewart, Michael Jordan and many more sports legends at a charity golf tournament.

1990-1994 — After moving to Roseburg, Oregon, I passed my real estate exam, took a short-lived job at a real-estate company owned by Jerry Chartier, from whom I learned some valuable business and life lessons. I became severely depressed, experiencing severe panic attacks almost daily. I feel these panic attacks stemmed from a severe allergic reaction that nearly took my life in 1986 while attending college in Texas. I passed my RPT exams to become a fully registered piano technician.

1994-1995 — Divorce! With two failed marriages, I felt like a complete and total failure... My depression, anxiety and panic attacks are now consuming my life. I am no longer the man I once was. I have no clue what, where, or why I am in this place.

1995-1998 — I continued to struggle with panic attacks, anxiety, and fear, but knew I must try to carry on with life. I started trading stocks online and sold baseball cards on eBay on a regular basis to supplement my income. I also stepped into the network marketing business world, selling jewelry and experiencing my first taste of financial success.

1998-2001 – I met Olé Dayle Maloney, who became my first real mentor for success. I was soon traveling around the country on business trips that forced me to face my fears and anxiety. While attending these events for the company I was working with, I also learned many valuable lessons that would bode well for my future successes. Chauffeurs held my name on signs at airports and escorted me to 5-star hotels in limousines to attend conferences for the new network marketing company that I joined.

2001-2002 — Unfortunately, my life unravels once again. I must break down this monumental time in my life into stages.

May 2001 — My dad passed away.

September 2001 — On 9-11, our country is rocked by the attacks on the World Trade Center. My piano service business suffers greatly thereafter.

October 2001 — With the hassles of travel after 9/11, my life began to unravel. I decided to leave the network marketing business to focus on being a dad to my kids and saving my piano service business from going under.

December – 2001 — I was in shock when the piano store where I worked closed their doors for good. My security and income spiraled downward.

2002-2003 — Life is difficult to say the least. Drowning in debt and barely paying my monthly bills, I am deeply depressed and starting to feel the pain of leaving the network marketing business world. However, I had no fire within to make the sacrifices to work hard enough to go back. My kids have become far more important!

2003-2004 — As my piano service business continues to fail, I become increasingly more depressed, broke, and tired. I wanted to run with my kids to Texas where I had attended college and had friends, believing that starting somewhere new would help me escape the pain. However, I knew deep down that running from my problems would likely not fix anything. By the end of 2004, I filed for bankruptcy.

2004-2005 — I lost almost everything in my finalized bankruptcy. To make ends meet, I take a job selling cars and enjoy my co-workers, but I quickly discovered that I was not cut out for selling cars. However, that short time in a job **I was not created for** made me want to work harder and develop the disciplines to really achieve my best dreams and live the life I WAS created for.

2005-2007 — With a new mindset, more drive, and a grip on my panic attacks, my piano service business slowly regained momentum. Taking my son Andrew on a camping/fishing trip proved to be a monumental step in my battle against my panic attacks and fear. I still suffered occasional panic attacks and anxiety, but they have become almost nonexistent in my life.

2007-2008 — January 19, 2007, the passing of my eldest sister Sharlene from cancer left a HUGE hole in my heart, but I was determined to be successful and get back on top. In late 2007 the Edward Jones Financial Services company hired me to train to become a financial advisor. I had enjoyed a love for the stock market for many years and this position was a dream come true... or so I thought.

2008-2009 — Although I loved trading stocks personally, I soon discovered I did not have a fire burning within to pursue a career in the financial industry. I quit my job with Edward Jones and began focusing on building my piano service business. I discovered online marketing with Google AdSense and slowly built a profitable online business writing articles and building small websites to supplement my income. This business was only a means to pay the bills—not a passion or dream.

2009-2010 — The Internet was changing, and I was steadily falling behind in maintaining my online following through writing articles. I lacked the fire. Thankfully, my piano service business was still supporting me. I continued with my online stock trading and investing, though I was not that successful.

2010-2011 — These years mark another extremely pivotal time in my life... My finances and mental state were still far from where I needed them to be. I was getting by, but I needed to supplement my income. I had always dreamed of being in full-time ministry but felt I did not qualify. However, I found amazing pastors, Randy and Lisa Scroggins, who gave me a try in a part-time church position as an administrator. I thought administrating was my dream job as well but found I lacked the fire I needed to find my best dreams. Thinking that marriage would bring me the elusive happiness I was searching for, I met a beautiful woman online, proposed, and married her. Four months later, my third marriage ended in divorce. Completely devastated, I felt I must be a total loser with dwindling finances, failed marriages, and struggling business ventures. Thankfully, the church did not fire me, voting instead to support me and help me regain my dignity.

2011-2012 — The times when I thought I should give up, I had friends, family, and a good church behind me. Although I struggled emotionally and financially again, I kept pressing on. Life was not great, and I was not where I wanted to be, but I was determined to find answers and continue searching for my best dreams.

2012-2013 — Another devastating setback came with a diagnosis of type 2 diabetes. For a short time, I was practically blind and lost 40 pounds. The unthinkable happened when my son Andrew was stabbed in a street fight. The doctor who operated on Andrew told me months later that as a trained surgeon, he could not have stabbed my son with any more precision. Had the wound been mere eyelashes to the left or the right, he would not have survived. That frightening, but miraculous, time led to my son's turning his life around. He is now a wonderful man and father today.

2013-2014 — Once again, I started to make progress in my mindset and attitude in life. I became determined to chase my best dreams regardless of the train wreck I had made of my life. Late 2013 I recorded a solo piano CD. I also decided to step away from my position at the church to pursue new ventures in life. I focused all my energy into my piano service business. I remained determined to chase my best dreams and passions to inspire others to NEVER GIVE UP.

2014-2015 — A Portland piano store owner named Mitch Paola allowed me to open and manage a piano store for him in Eugene where I had grown up. Traveling an hour to work was a grind, but I was driven to succeed. I also became a grandfather for the first time as well.

2015-2017 — I struggled to keep the piano store going, but the fire was still burning inside me to chase my best dreams and succeed. The going was extremely difficult, and I was almost ready to give up. Knowing I had to keep pressing on, I started journalling regularly. The process helped me sort out my thoughts and ideas in writing so I could chart my daily progress. I received a call from Beth, who was interested in purchasing a higher-end grand piano. That call started a remarkable run of piano sales.

2017-2018 — I made several life changes, including moving the piano store to a new location in hopes of taking the store to a new level of success. A friend offered me a place in Springfield, so I moved to that area to be closer to my work, pressed hard to improve my stock trading skills, to build the piano store, and develop my piano service business.

2018-2019 — In September of 2018 as I was beginning on a new path to greater successes, my mother's journey on earth was ending. I became very intentional about investing and swing trading stocks on a regular basis. Changing my stock trading mindset began paying off nicely. The piano store started to gain momentum as well, which boosted my piano service business too. I started attending a good church, Mannahouse, and became good friends with Ken Elliott.

2019-2021 — I bought stock in a company called Novavax (NVAX). The worldwide pandemic was moving through our world, bringing many changes. My stock NVAX soars to the moon on hopes of a new vaccine, which gives me the confidence and financial means to invest even more time and energy into my stock trading and investing. Life is changing for me as well—for the better.

A new chapter is about to take off in my life—authoring four books: the *Quick Charge Your Life* series (three books), and *Swim with the Sharks: Outsmart the Market*. My stock trading and investing are going extremely well, my piano service business is booming, and piano sales are also going exceedingly well—all during some crazy times for the world.

2021-to present — Life is FAR from perfect, but it's about as good as I could ever imagine. I am working on this book about discovering your best dreams and igniting the fire within, but I do not yet know the title. I have built a thriving, successful piano service business, the piano store I manage is doing well, and I have finally tapped into my best dreams of authoring books to inspire others. I love the thrill of stock trading, but 2022 has been a tough year for a stock trader or at least for me, but I have a fire burning deep within to win in the markets.

End of Timeline
(to be continued...)

I am FAR from done! I know life is an uphill climb. I am sure I'll have some more setbacks along the way. But when I look back over all the life that I have travelled through I know the key is in pressing on and never giving up despite all my mistakes and setbacks I have encountered.

> "*Failure will never overtake me if my determination to succeed is strong enough.*"

> – OG MANDINO

So, am I happier today? Yes—happier, fulfilled, and more successful—but not because of the successes in my life.

Yes, I am happier and more fulfilled because of my discipline and drive to never give up!

Yes, I am happier, fulfilled, and more successful today because I have finally discovered that the keys to happiness and success are in being disciplined to choose happiness every single day that I wake up as I work to add value to others.

Yes, I am happier, fulfilled, and more successful today because I understand that everything good in life is uphill.

Yes, I am happier, fulfilled, and more successful today because I intentionally live out my *Quick Charge Life* concept and Secret Sauce Formula.

I still have days when I struggle to get there. Life and success will ALWAYS be an uphill climb! But the view from where I stand now is much better than where I stood a few short years ago on my life's journey.

As you can see by my timeline. I have failed miserably at times. I have hurt people in the past. I am still far from perfect and never will arrive at perfection. I have had some tremendous setbacks and challenges in my life's journey; however, I am more driven, intentional, and disciplined with my life today than ever before! I am focused on serving and adding value to others. I am only successful today because the Lord is gracious, merciful, loving, and incredibly forgiving.

"Do not judge me by my successes, judge me by how many times I fell down and got back up again."

— NELSON MANDELA

"In order to write about life, first you must live it."

— ERNEST HEMINGWAY

SECTION THREE

Develop Your Discipline

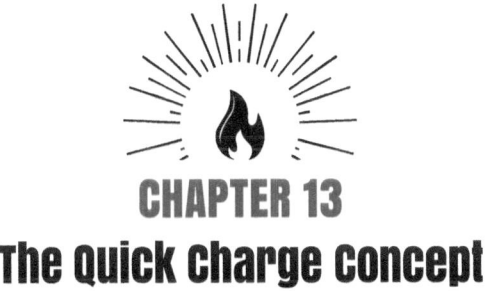

CHAPTER 13
The Quick charge concept

Sadly, millions of people in this world go to work every day and stay in that job for decades or more but feel lost, unfulfilled, and stuck. Instead of developing the proper mindset and discipline to find the path they are designed to be on, they decide to accept their life. They take what has been handed to them instead of going after what they really want in life. Many people accept a job or choose a career path that pays the bills. However, that career does not ignite a fire within to develop the proper mindset and disciplines to succeed.

Immediately employing the following two practices is of utmost importance:

- Develop the proper mindset.
- Develop a set of disciplines that fit your life's design.

Understanding the power of these two simple principles will allow you to move forward with the proper directions for your life. The next section of this book will help you understand, develop, and employ these two principles.

Do you feel stuck in your current career? Are you unhappy about where you are in life? Do you feel there has to be more to life if you could just discover it? I have been where you are. You may need to simply rewire your thoughts and start moving in the direction of developing a new mindset. You may need to practice a personalized set of disciplines until the path is clear. I am speaking from experience as I make these suggestions.

I have mentioned the *Quick Charge Concept* several times in this book, and I would like to share the structure of this approach that empowers individuals to align their faith and positive mindset with the success and happiness they deserve. Having the proper mindset goes hand in hand with the proper discipline.

The *Quick Charge Concept* embraces the following intangibles:

#1 Faith
- Develop a personal relationship with the Lord and continually seek Him to energize you with His power.

#2 Happiness

- Take responsibility for your happiness by thinking positive thoughts—no matter what you may encounter in life.

#3 Confidence | Passion

- Invest in yourself and create a personal *secret sauce formula* to reach your goals and dreams.

#4 Wealth | Stability | Freedom

- Invest smarter, be diversified, and build your wealth.

#5 Peace

- Learn to be calm and trust the Lord during the storms of life.

#6 Balance

- Create life balance by generously giving of all that God has given you.

#7 Joy | Fulfillment

- Find joy and fulfillment in serving, adding value to, and inspiring others.

In a nutshell, The *Quick Charge* concept is an invitation for you to change the way you think intentionally, deliberately, and consciously. As a result, you might well discover all the *quick-charge* outlets God surrounds you with every single day of your life. The *Quick-Charge* concept will allow you to continually charge the power already within you to look past your perceived limitations and boldly step into the life you were born to create.

Learn it, live it, and inspire others...
Quick Charge Your Life!

> *"Positive thinking is powerful thinking. If you want happiness, fulfillment, success and inner peace, start thinking you have the power to achieve those things. Focus on the bright side of life and expect positive results."*
>
> – GERMANY KENT

The Secret Sauce Formula

A few years ago, when I created the *Quick-Charge Concept,* I also developed what I like to call my personal "Secret Sauce Formula" for success and happiness. The truth is, there are no BIG secrets to finding success in life. Anyone can create his own Secret Sauce Formula. However, checking out a *secret* seems to gain more attention and inspires more people than something that always has been right in front of them!

As I reveal my personal "Secret-Sauce-Formula" concoction, take into consideration that your personal Secret-Sauce-Formula ingredients will be different from mine.

> *The greatest mistake you can make in life is to be continually fearing you will make one.*
>
> – ELBERT HUBBARD

Your Secret Sauce Formula

Your **Secret Sauce Formula** is your personal concoction of **daily disciplines** to which you must adhere to daily, weekly, and monthly. Several of the ingredients that you will choose to create your Secret Sauce will be used daily. Other ingredients might be used every other day or a couple of times each week. However, may I encourage you to practice using as many of the ingredients in your secret sauce concoction as possible every single day of the week in order to create a powerful mixture. The ingredients in your secret sauce formula may change over time, but you must create a formula that works for you personally and then begin to apply as many ingredients as you can to your life every single day.

The best way to understand how your **Secret Sauce Formula** will help you is by seeing it as a **toolkit** that you will carry with you through life. By applying a daily set of disciplines (your **Secret Sauce Formula**), you will gain the wisdom, knowledge, strength, and skills you need to achieve whatever goals and dreams you have set for yourself.

I do hope you will realize exactly how powerful this formula can be to achieving anything you desire in life. The following 11.7 ingredients comprise my personal "Secret Sauce Formula." The Roman numerals represent my eleven main ingredients, and I use standard numbers for what I call the seven sub-ingredients.

I. Make my bed.

II. Pray.
1. Devotional reading

III. Speak positive words into my life.
2. Express gratitude and thankfulness.
3. Inspire others.

IV. File ideas, quotes, articles, videos, jokes, book clips.

V. Research.
4. Listen to podcasts, watch educational and inspirational videos.

VI. Think and listen.
5. Ask questions (God, myself, and others).
6. Listen to the Holy Spirit and people.

VII. Read and listen every day.
7. Bible, nonfiction inspirational books, nonfiction audio books, articles, podcast, and blogs.

VIII. Laugh often.

IX. Exercise daily.

X. Eat healthy.

XI. Journal my thoughts, ideas, and personal accounts of each day.

I frequently engage in additional activities, but I do not consider them regular disciplines, habits, and hobbies. My enjoyable extras include golfing, fishing, attending Oregon Duck sporting events, concerts, bowling, traveling, relaxing, photography, hiking, playing piano, spending time with friends and family.

Each person will have a different mix of ingredients for his or her Secret Sauce Formula. As you can see, I have eleven main ingredients and seven sub-ingredients that I focus on for my personal Secret Sauce Formula, thus the "11.7."

As you create your Secret Sauce Formula, one key to consider is not trying to think of all your ingredients at once. You can add, change, and mix more ingredients into the sauce as you continue... I started with only five main ingredients and one sub-ingredient. I continued to add more until I now have more than doubled my ingredients. You may have more than 11.7 ingredients or only a few for your Secret Sauce Formula for success. I feel a good recipe mix should include at least 3.1 to 12.9 ingredients.

It's time to create your personal **Secret Sauce Formula**!

The key is to choose daily disciplines and activities that will bring you closer to your goals and best dreams in life. These disciplines and activities you choose to adhere to daily, weekly, and monthly will carry you to success. The following are some ingredient suggestions to add to your **Secret Success Formula**. You might want to choose to include some of the following:

> Reading, making your bed, jogging, hiking, research, studying, working out, writing, filing, singing, learning a foreign language, typing, walking, cooking, fishing, golf, swimming, thinking, asking questions, traveling, public speaking, listening to podcasts, watching videos, blogging, engaging in personal Bible study, devotionals, meeting new people, karate,

judo, yoga, meditation, relaxation, painting, drawing, playing piano or another musical instruments, sewing, knitting, photography, bird watching, gardening, dancing, woodworking, laughing, showing gratefulness, watching comedies, volunteering, and much more...

The list of options to include in your Secret Sauce Formula mix is endless! Keep in mind that you may wish to add or change some ingredients over time to create the perfect formula for your life as you climb to success.

"An investment in knowledge pays the best interest."
— BENJAMIN FRANKLIN

"Instead of worrying about what you cannot control, shift your energy to what you can create."
— ROY T. BENNETT

CHAPTER 14
It's Time to Journal

Keeping a regular journal can be powerful and impactful to your success. Many books highly regard and value the benefits of journaling. Videos on YouTube recognize the power of journaling. Many successful and highly driven people will go out of their way to emphasize how important journaling is to their life and success.

> *"Journal writing gives us insights into who we are, who we were, and who we can become."*
> – SANDRA MARINELLA

I am one more voice who will yell from the mountaintops about how vitally important and life-changing journaling is to my life. The practice has impacted me for the better and has helped me to keep pressing on. I cannot say journaling is the answer or the key to the success I have enjoyed. I will argue that since I began journaling consistently, the exercise has played a huge role on my ability to develop the disciplines that have led to the successes in my life.

I absolutely credit journaling as the key catalyst to starting my journey and igniting the fire in me for authoring books. While journaling my thoughts, I discovered how much writing lights a fire in me to author more books. Therefore, I decided to specifically devote a chapter to my discipline and love for journaling.

Journaling is a major ingredient in my Secret Sauce Formula of disciplines. I discipline myself to jot a few thoughts, ideas, and notes into my life journal almost every day. However, I did notice one startling pattern as I was reading back through several of my journal posts. During 2021 and early 2022, I had gaps lasting for days and sometime weeks where I did not journal at all. That pattern became even more evident as I continued to look through notes from June of 2021 to February of 2022. I realized that during some of my less productive times in life, I had made mention of how my motivation was not as on fire to maintain all that I had happening.

What I saw worth noting was that I had not backed off completely from pushing myself to keep driving in the other interests in my life. I was still pressing on and practicing some of the disciplines in my Secret Sauce Formula. After all, I had authored four books in 18 months, spanning from early 2019 into early 2021. As I read my journal notes, I specifically noticed in a few entries that I did not want to slow down on authoring more books. However, I had done nothing to continue pursuing that goal; I had not been working on any new book project ideas.

Although I was busy doing many things, I was leaving out some important aspects of what fuels me. I was not being consistent to stay in touch with my goals, dreams, and visions that I had recorded in my journal for pursuing my passion of writing more books!

Fast forward to March of 2022. I saw a real change in my discipline. I saw a consistent record of almost daily notes in my journal once again. I may have missed a day or two at a time here and there, but I saw much more consistency and passion in my posts. I noticed around May of 2022 that I started inputting daily entries in my journal with barely any missed days. Remarkably, I also started to gain momentum in my attitude toward writing, success, and re-igniting my passion of authoring more books and inspiring others to chase after their dreams. The creative juices started flowing and new ideas and thoughts for another book project—the one you are reading now.

I am not the smartest guy in the room, but seeing the correlation between my discipline of consistently journaling my thoughts and my accelerated momentum toward chasing my goal of starting a new book project did not take me long. Yes, I could absolutely see that when I was disciplined to journal daily, I was quickly gaining momentum in life to push myself again to write more. Seeing your thoughts, ideas, and notes in raw form in a journal can remotivate you again!

You might be wondering how I journal. Hopefully, you will also want to know how you can start using this incredible discipline to move toward your greatest life design.

The following are some keys I like to apply when I journal:

- Do not take the time to edit your journal notes. They should be raw and unedited.
- Record the dates of each post so you can track the timeline.
- Take the time to look back over your journal notes at times.
- When you are recording a thought, do not stop to read back over it. Simply keep writing until you run out of words to express your thoughts for that entry.
- Throw out the rules and journal however you feel will best help you to keep driving forward to reach your goals in life.

Some personal insights that I have had on my journaling journey might be of help to you. I started randomly journaling in 2009, and sadly, I did not even start dating my posts consistently until 2018. Between the years of 2009 to 2016, I really have no idea what year or what days many of my older journal posts take place. I know I started journaling in 2009 because I happened to find some older dated notes that matched the first records I found in my journal.

Looking back now and seeing the track records of some of my early thoughts as I worked through big decisions in my life is amazing. I had placed such importance on some of those decisions that turned out not to matter nearly as much or at all in the end. When I recorded my thoughts at the time, it was a big deal.

What's even more incredible is all the life that I have lived—good, bad, and ugly—and how much life has changed for me since 2009. Reading back over my early thoughts and ideas, I find it difficult to believe that I am the same person I read about in the entries from 2009 to 2014.

How to Keep a Record of Your Journal Thoughts

Many people use a pen to record in a regular lined journal. However, I do not have great handwriting, so I chose to use my computer and a word-processing program. I personally use two programs to keep a record of my journal notes: Microsoft Word and an app called Notes on my iPhone. I transfer the notes from my iPhone to my Microsoft Word file on my computer. You can do a quick search online for word-processing programs to find the best ones for you.

One note on editing: do not stop recording your thoughts. Keep going with your thoughts until the thought is completed. You can then reread and make needed corrections. Do not try to make it read pretty or as if the text will be graded or read by others. I think it is best to leave it raw. Just record the way you feel and leave it at that.

If you do not like to type or write, then use a text-to-speech app to talk out your thoughts, ideas, and feelings into a microphone or headset. Your words will *magically* flow onto the page... I do this at times when I do not feel like typing, but I normally enjoy the sound and the feel of keystrokes as I record my thoughts and ideas for the day.

If you have not already started a daily journal, then I strongly encourage you to make this practice one of your top priorities in the main ingredients of disciplines in your secret sauce formula. If you have already started a journal, then I hope this chapter inspires you to continue journaling with intention. The discipline to journal daily will carry you through to helping you with disciplines in other areas of your life as well.

Happy journaling...

> *"Your journal is like your best friend; you don't have to pretend with it, you can be honest and write exactly how you feel."*
>
> — BUKOLA OGUNWALE

CHAPTER 15
It Takes a Village

Over the past year or so, Ken Elliott has become one of my very best friends. We spend endless hours talking about our passions in life which include golfing, stock trading, and serving the Lord. He has become one of God's blessings in my life.

Visiting with Ken reminds me of the importance of surrounding myself with good people. I have learned that a good team of friends and business associates will help you to stay accountable and disciplined to achieve your goals. You can share your dreams and goals with your TEAM, and they can encourage you when you need a little boost.

As I have been working on this book, I have been challenged to really press in and continue sharing my thoughts, ideas, and messages with the world through the vehicle of authoring books. I know that accomplishing all the goals and best dreams that I have planted inside of me will take much work and perseverance. Therefore, surrounding myself with good people who will support me and help me get to the next level is essential.

> *"The size of your team will determine
> the size of your dream."*
>
> – JOHN MAXWELL

I love this quote about the size of your team by John Maxwell. I do believe this quote is targeted more toward building a strong team in a corporate setting, but having a team can be equally important in building your personal business relationships and personal friendships as well.

This concept of building a team made me think about the size of my team. I have now become more intentional about surrounding myself with a network of superb people. Connecting and building relationships with good people to whom I can add value and serve has become a new challenge for me.

Placing an abundance of emphasis on the value of serving others and adding value to another's life is essential to an individual's success. If you seek out others to whom you can bring value and serve, then you will in turn find a strong team of individuals to support your dreams and goals.

On the other hand, if you have negative people in your life who are always pulling you down, then you will likely never get to where you really want to be. Walking away from some relationships may be difficult, but surrounding yourself with people who will build you up and support you is essential.

> *"You can love them, forgive them, want good things
> for them...but still move on without them."*
>
> – MANDY HALE

I have been much more purposeful and careful about who I add to my team these past few years. I am continually adding valuable new members to my team such as my wonderful pastor, Bryan Wheelon, who has become a good friend to me. He frequently sends a meaningful text at just the right time to let me know he is thinking about me, wanting to uplift me, and wishing me the best.

I have never personally met others on my team, but we have exchanged hundreds of emails, multiple phone calls, zoom calls, and shared endless thoughts and ideas as I build my book-authoring business.

I do not talk to several business-related friends as often as I would like, but I know they always have my back and support me in all my endeavors. Two lifelong friends, Dave Osban and Robert New, have been with me through most of my good times, bad times, mistakes, and everything in between in my adult life. They have always remained in my corner regardless of whether I was succeeding or failing.

I am blessed with some lifelong college friends, Dan Belles, Janet Rowland, and Saya Benitez. We don't see each other often or talk as frequently these days, but if I needed help, I know I could call on any of them at any time.

I am continuing to seek the Lord as I build my team of individuals and business relationships on whom I can lean, learn from, pray with, discuss ideas with, laugh with, cry with, and hopefully I can serve and add value to their lives along the way as well.

> *"Find a group of people who challenge and inspire you; spend a lot of time with them, and it will change your life."*
> — AMY POEHLER

Who is on your team? Do you have people with whom you can be open and honest? Do you have people in your life to whom you can go when you are struggling? Can you count on them to lift you up and help you to get back in the driver's seat to press on toward your goals and dreams?

Being careful not to add people to your team who will agree with everything you do and not hold you accountable is an important consideration. You will want strong supporters who are not afraid to make suggestions when they feel you are out of line.

How much time do you spend networking and building business relationships? I learned many years ago the value of exchanging contact information with business associates. When I am ready to make a business deal or need to bounce a business idea off them, I can call them for advice.

If you could put a number on it, how many people do you want or need on your team to help you reach your biggest goals and dreams? As I typed that last sentence, I almost deleted it because I do not feel that assigning a number to how many people you want or need in your corner is possible. If you are good at networking, then you should build as big a team as you possibly can.

I plan to keep building a BIG team...I have very BIG DREAMS! I feel it is essential to always be looking to add new people to our team. I am making a lifelong goal to keep adding people to my team to whom I can add value and serve.

> *"You need to associate with people that inspire you, people that challenge you to rise higher, people that make you better. Don't waste your valuable time with people that are not adding to your growth. Your destiny is too important."*
> – JOEL OSTEEN

SECTION FOUR

Determine Your Drive

CHAPTER 16
Are We There Yet?

For anyone who has ever taken a road trip or vacation with younger children, you have probably heard the most-often-asked question in life: ***"Are we there yet?"*** Sometimes kids will ask this same question five minutes into a long trip...and every five minutes thereafter!

When it comes to chasing your best dreams and developing the disciplines to drive for success in life, this most-often-asked question, "Are we there yet?" comes into play. And the answer is NO! We are NOT there yet... Thinking success is a destination is one of the first false ideas and mindset mistakes that we must adjust to focus on the right path.

If you are still asking, "Are we there yet?" then you are asking the wrong question!

One of the purposes of this book is to help you understand that the common thread burning inside anyone who has experienced lasting success is that they never stop driving themselves to do more, serve more, challenge themselves more, learn more, and continually add more value to others... They keep driving on to the next level of success.

> *"Success is not a destination; it is a wonderful, ongoing journey of adding value to people and serving others."*
>
> – TOMMY TURNER

Recently I was watching a podcast on YouTube by Ed Mylett, who invited Dr. John Maxwell, one of my all-time favorite authors, speakers, teachers, and business leaders to be on his podcast. John shared several profound thoughts, and I want to highlight a couple of his incredibly impactful ideas to help develop this chapter.

One very profound thought that really brings this chapter into focus John shared gave me a tremendous *Quick Charge*. John said that *everything worthwhile is uphill*. Nothing in your life is *not* an uphill effort. He continued, "The problem with most people is that they have uphill hopes, but downhill habits."

> *"Everything worthwhile is uphill. The problem is, we have downhill habits. If you have downhill habits and you have uphill hopes, you're in trouble."*
>
> – JOHN MAXWELL

Toward the conclusion of the podcast, Ed Mylett asked John, "If someone approached you in a coffee shop and asked, 'Mr. Maxwell, could I have a minute of your time? What steps would you tell me to take to transform my life?' what would you share with that person?"

Being a man of faith, John first said he would share about His relationship with God. "When you have something wonderful, you just want to share it." He said he would not judge a person who had no interest in a relationship with God; he would love that person just the same. Dr. Maxwell mentioned his faith because he gives all credit first to the Lord for all he has and having faith in Christ Who transformed his life.

I love this thought because that is exactly how I feel about my faith with the Lord. I will always profess my love for Him in everything that I do whether it be authoring a book or talking with someone about life because I would be nowhere without the Lord in my life. However, I will never force my faith on someone else or judge anyone who does not believe the way I do.

John Maxwell also shared that if you really want to be transformed, then you must live an intentional life, saying, "Most people don't *lead* their life; they *accept* their life." He emphasized that being intentional is so simple; "Don't miss the truth. If you accept your life, you are simply living on things not worthy of your time, effort, and energy."

I briefly touched on a similar thought when I addressed finding the BEST seeds planted within you. If you are simply accepting your life, then chances are you are not focused on the best dreams planted within you.

I've already mentioned John Maxwell's statement that everything worthwhile in life is uphill, and to go uphill, you must be intentional! Nobody ever went uphill by accident. I can't imagine ever reading a book on accidental achievements! In other words, we must be intentional with what we do and who we are.

Going back to the person who might ask what steps he could take to transform his life, Dr. Maxwell said he would tell the person to find his strengths, become very intentional, and commit his life every day to the uphill journey. Keep Driving...

No matter how much influence you may have or how talented or wealthy or famous you are, the real focus of this point is that you still must go uphill. <u>Everyone.</u> Must. Go. Uphill. The greatest mistake that we make in life is to think *I am just going to go out, make enough money to relax, and then live happily ever after.* However, the day you reach this place, then you are really missing the point.

If you are alive, then life still goes on, and no matter who you are, trials will come. Perhaps one of your loved ones is involved in a terrible accident or something else tragic happens in your life, and no matter your level of success or wealth, heartbreaks will cause pain and often confusion as to why.

My point is that problems will never leave you. You will have issues, obstacles, and difficulties along the way. Anything worth having is an uphill battle. Struggles will always come across your path.

So, I want to bring this point made by John Maxwell around full circle apply it to the question this chapter is emphasizing: "Are We There Yet?"

Dr. Maxwell's ultimate point and the main point of this chapter is to understand that you never get to the place where you've "got it made." You are not supposed to have it made. While we are living on this earth, we will never be there yet! We are supposed to keep pressing on and adding value to people until we have no life left to give.

Because I believe this point goes even deeper, I would like to add that we are also to serve people. If you want to feel the greatest form of success and happiness, then stop trying to find the easy button! Start serving others and adding value to them.

Once you understand this simple principle of adding value to people and serving others, then you will develop the proper mindset and discipline to keep driving uphill with intention and boundless joy. What's wonderful about going uphill is that the higher your climb, the scenery gets better and better!

The last point John Maxwell mentioned in that interview was *good intentions are overrated.* We can have all the good intentions and dreams in the world, but we must change our good intentions into good actions. Nothing happens with our good intentions until we have good actions and disciplines. We will not develop good actions and disciplines until we live an intentional life.

My friend, you must get in the vehicle of success, turn the key, and start driving with intention. Your discipline will come as you understand what and where it is you are meant to be in life.

> *"Do you want to have an easy life? Then always stay with the herd and lose yourself in the herd."*
> — FRIEDRICH NIETZSCHE

> *"Chains of habit are too light to be felt until they are too heavy to be broken."*
> — WARREN BUFFETT

CHAPTER 17
Life in a Nutshell

I was watching an interview the other day featuring the famous investor, Warren Buffett. I was amazed at this 92-year-old's passion, his continued drive for success, and his love for his work. Not only does Mr. Buffett love going to work every day, he also enjoys speaking, doing interviews, and imparting his investment knowledge to others! In other words, he still loves adding value to others every single day that he is able.

I can totally identify with Mr. Buffett's passion and drive for getting up and working every day. I must admit, at 62 years *young*, I never feel like I work a day in my life! I do not have tomorrow promised to me, and the fact is, no one does. However, for as long as I am alive, I do not see myself wanting to fully retire or slow down to a crawl. I want to keep pressing on everyday—like Warren Buffett.

"Without passion, you don't have energy.
Without energy, you have nothing."

– WARREN BUFFETT

I have so much joy, passion, energy, and excitement for all the opportunities and businesses in which I invest my time and efforts every single day. I want to keep driving toward more goals and dreams for the rest of my life.

> *I want to climb so high up my ladder of success in life that I have no more steps left to climb. That is when I will reach up and take the hands of Jesus as He pulls me up into heaven. That is when I can rest and enjoy an eternity filled with more joy, love, and blessings than I can ever imagine. I want to hear the Lord say, "Well done, My good and faithful servant."*
> – TOMMY TURNER

I realize that not everyone will have the same faith as I do or the same disciplines, goals, and aspirations as I do. For those who know they have a unique drive for success in life like I do, I want to let you know that you are not alone. Millions of people around the world have a similar drive, passion, and energy inside for giving all they can to serve and add value to others.

What exactly is serving and adding value to people?

I am reminded of a teaching moment in my life from many years ago when I was not aware of the importance of adding value to others. I would like to share an example of what it means to add value.

This "value-adding moment" came about in the early 90s while I was selling real estate in Roseburg, Oregon, for a company owned by Jerry Chartier. Jerry and I were across the street from the office eating lunch, and our waitress asked us if we wanted coffee. I was busy reading my menu, and without looking at her, I replied, "No." After the waitress walked away, Jerry taught me about adding value to another person's life.

He said, "Tom, you never even looked at her. What if she walks into the office looking to buy a home, and you are the person who is up on the floor for the next lead. She might remember that you never even took the time to acknowledge her at the restaurant and decide to go somewhere else. She might even request to work with someone else."

Jerry's talk reminded me that we should always value people by taking the time to look at them, smile, and speak. I don't always do well at **acknowledging** people, but I do value that lesson he taught me many years ago and try to do my best. *Thanks, Jerry.*

No matter what you do in life, you can serve and add value to others.

- Perhaps you are a contractor who builds homes. Serve others by doing your very best, go the extra mile, and try to do even more. Take the time to acknowledge your crew and let them know they matter.
- Are you a daycare provider? Honor the kids who are placed in your care. In doing so, you are serving them and their parents who entrusted their children to you.
- If you are in any kind of service business, do your job to the best of your abilities and always remember the value of your customers. This is a wonderful way to serve and add value.
- If you are a teacher, you can add value and serve your students every day by teaching them with integrity and honesty. Instill values into the lives of your students by listening, caring, and helping them to go beyond the classroom to be a better human being.
- If you are a doctor, pay closer attention to each patient's needs and situation. When you feel tired and stressed, then take a step back and remember the value and the influence you have over someone's life by your words and expertise when they are under your care.

- If you are a ____ [fill in the blank], do your tasks with passion, integrity, and intention! If your job requires you to talk and interact with others, then listen and show them how much they matter. You can make the difference and add value to another person's life every day just by having great intention.

In doing a quick Google search on adding value to others, the following are the results:

- Show value through your gestures that you are there for him or her.
- Make time.
- Give someone your full attention.
- Give a hug.
- Show that you're listening.
- Offer a gift.
- Help.
- Care deeply.

I wish I could say that I have understood these values forever, but I have had to learn the hard way over the years by making too many mistakes. I will admit that I have days when I am not so good at adding value to others. I do a little better some days. However, I am much better at it when I discipline myself to take the time to remind myself of the importance of adding value and serving others with intention.

> *"The purpose of human life is to serve, and to show compassion and the will to help others."*
> – ALBERT SCHWEITZER

"Everyone has a purpose in life and a unique talent to give to others. And when we blend this unique talent with service to others, we experience the ecstasy and exultation of our spirit, which is the ultimate goal of all goals."

— KALLAM ANJI REDDY

CHAPTER 18
In What Group Are You?

Statistics say that nearly 80 percent of people do not achieve a life of success or live the life they dream of living. Only 20 percent are doers and succeed at living a better life. However, only 8 percent of people live their *best* dreams, and if you drill down even deeper, only 5 percent become the highest achievers of this world.

You may not have dreams and desires to be one of the 8 percent or even one of the 5 percent of high achievers in the world. I do believe that the percentage number we should all be striving for should be much higher than the top 20 percent. Everyone was put on this earth to live an extraordinary life! Yes, every person is born to create and live a successful life.

If you truly have a fire burning inside to live your dream life, then you must set your goals outrageously high—as if you were aiming for the top 5 percent. If you fail to reach your outrageous goals, you are more likely to be much closer to falling into the top 20 percent who are successful. Possibly you will even reach the 8 percent who are extremely successful. Maybe you will surprise yourself and reach the 5 percent high achievers' level and become outrageously successful one day.

I do have extremely outrageous goals set for myself to achieve. Reaching all of them will likely take me two lifetimes, but I like to aim high. I live my life very focused on reaching an extremely outrageous 5-percent-level territory. I may never get there, but I know that having BIG goals and dreams will allow me to go much higher than I would have if I had only set easy-to-attain goals.

So, what does a person who is in the 8-percent club do to get there? They work harder, longer, smarter, and more intentionally than other 92 percenters. They have a few close personal relationships, and they are always building and networking to create powerful personal and business relationships. I also believe their calling is to be at this higher level.

> *"Highly motivated achievers are looking not to receive but to contribute. They are looking for problems that are personally satisfying to solve."*
> – DENIS WAITLEY

Although most high achievers may not know of my Secret Sauce Formula, I can assure you that anyone who is living a successful life in the 20-percent realm or higher has created their own concoction of a Secret Sauce Formula they follow on a strict basis.

When I think of the five percent of high achievers in this world, I have an image in my mind of a fighter jet. Above that jet, I see a large cargo carrier (the jet's support team) carrying aviation kerosene to refuel the jet in midair. The support team keeps the jet in flight so they do not lose travel time.

Highly successful people have mastered the disciplines to manage their time, money, diet, and life habits very strictly. You must have a raging fire within for success to become a high achiever. You must be all in when it comes to continuing to drive toward higher goals and bigger dreams.

I do not know of any high achiever or any highly successful person who is perfect. We all make mistakes and face uphill challenges in life. However, the difference in the mindset of the 20 percent who succeed is that they have the drive and determination to succeed and add more value to others.

People who live intentionally and enjoy more successes in life will develop the disciplines to get back up and carry on. Anytime high achievers fail at something on their journey to the next level of success, they learn from the failure instead of making an excuse as to why they did not or cannot make it.

I meet people all the time, and when I share my passion to inspire others, write books, trade stocks, service pianos, and all my other aspirations in life, I often hear the comment, "You have much more energy and drive than I do."

That observation is fine; however, that remark could mean any of the following rationalizations:

8. They are not willing to search for their best dreams, so they choose to accept their life.
9. They simply have not yet discovered their best dreams to ignite a fire within.
10. They are successful and perfectly happy with being in the 20-percent group and not interested in making a big splash.

Meeting someone in that 8-percent or 5-percent success group ignites the fire within me even more. They get the same boost of energy and excitement as well as we share our passions about life and success with one another.

Experiencing the undeniable energy and excitement of meeting someone who has achieved amazing accomplishments in life is something that you must experience to fully understand the power it brings. No words I speak or type can really express what an amazing feeling it is to connect with high achievers.

I conducted a quick Google search and discovered ten people who lived through failure before going on to become world-renowned names:

- Milton Hershey
- Albert Einstein
- Stephen King
- Thomas Edison
- Walt Disney
- Theodor (Dr. Seuss) Giesel
- Benjamin Franklin
- Oprah Winfrey
- Michael Jordan
- Abraham Lincoln

You may have no desire or ambition to become the next BIG name or high achiever but develop some disciplines and goals in your life as if your success depends on becoming one. I can assure you, my friend, you will go much higher than you can possibly dream or imagine right now! You must stay with it until you start seeing your dreams come true!

I watched an online video featuring the late great Jim Rohn, who was inspiring a room full of people to press on and never give up. The illustration he shared ignited a powerful *Quick Charge* in me that day I want to share.

He asked the audience a very simple question: "How long does a mother wait to see her baby walk?"

Does she reach a certain point and say, "Well, I guess it will never happen, so let's just forget about it"?

NO, she waits **UNTIL** the baby walks!

She will encourage the baby **UNTIL**. She continues to believe her baby can walk **UNTIL**. She simply encourages and waits **UNTIL** the baby totters a few steps.

Likewise, you can achieve anything you set your mind to. You can climb to your dreams and experience joy and success! So, how long will you wait to see your life in a new and powerful way?

UNTIL!

You can take everything that comes your way—good or bad—and use it to climb to your dreams and rise above **UNTIL** you achieve all your dreams and goals!

The great news is when it happens, it happens just like the baby suddenly learning to walk for the first time! Stay with it **UNTIL** it happens!

———

"High achievers spot rich opportunities swiftly, make big decisions quickly and move into action immediately. Follow these principles and you can make your dreams come true."

– ROBERT H. SCHULLER

"Your work is going to fill a large part of your life, and the only way to be truly satisfied is to do what you believe is great work. And the only way to do great work is to love what you do. If you haven't found it yet, keep looking. Don't settle. As with all matters of the heart, you'll know when you find it."

– STEVE JOBS

CHAPTER 19
What If?

As I begin this chapter, it is Christmas Day 2022. I rose early this morning, and I am so full of EXCITEMENT and HOPE for the day ahead of me. Yes, I am having a sweet *Quick Charge* moment. You might immediately assume that I have several wonderful presents wrapped under the tree, a pleasant time planned with family and eating enjoyable food for the day. Christmas days have normally been somewhat quiet for me these past several years.

Truthfully, the holiday season, in general and especially Christmas Eve and Christmas, are usually mellow days with some reflection and maybe a tear or two. I am always grateful for what this day represents; but for me, this season is not the same as it once was.

However, the Christmas season was not always that way... The holiday season used to be one of the most exciting times of the year for my family, but since my dad passed away in 2001 and then my sister Sharlene in 2007, holidays have never been the same.

My sister Sharlene was what we like to call "the glue of the family." She had an amazing way of making everything and everyone around her better. Not a day goes by that I do not miss her greatly. But on Christmas especially, I take time to think about what once was when she was alive, making everyone else's life a little bit better. She remains one of my biggest heroes!

My kids are all grown and usually spend the holidays with their kids on this day. I am good with their plans as we always find a special day to spend time celebrating the holidays together.

Most of my friends are also enjoying time with their loved ones as well. So, I normally take a drive to the coast or sit and read a good book. On this Christmas morning, I am feeling a little extra "pep in my step" as I work on the book you are reading right now.

Yes, it is Christmas Day, but rather than feeling the normal holiday blues, I am full of joy, hope, and passion. My mind is spinning with new ideas, thoughts, and optimism for what's to come. I really love days when I feel like this!

My mind is laser focused on all the good things that surround my life. Yes, I am so full of hope, joy, promise, and excitement today that I simply cannot stop thinking about it. I must admit, how I am feeling is far better than the alternative of feeling sad, hopeless, ungrateful, and defeated.

Thinking more about how I was feeling made me pose a question to myself: *why can't everyone feel this hopeful and optimistic every single day?*

One question led to another, and then I started asking more questions:

- What if someone had more money? Would it be easier for him or her to wake up and feel optimistic and hopeful every day?
- What if someone were in a wonderful relationship? Would he or she wake up every day feeling amazing and joyful?
- What if a couple had perfect kids? Would that make the difference?

- What if someone had the perfect job? Would all his or her troubles be over?
- What if someone had everything that he or she could possibly imagine? Would he or she then be able to reproduce this type of feeling every single minute of the day?

What If... Okay, I'm sure you are starting to get the point...

WHAT IF?

Isn't that the million-dollar question? Wouldn't it be great if I had the million-dollar answer too?

Well, Merry Christmas, I do have the million-dollar answer...

Wait! What did I just say?

Think back for a moment to the first thoughts you had when you read the words: *"**I do have the million-dollar answer.**"*

What did you feel inside? Don't worry! I will get to the million-dollar answer momentarily, but please take note of your feelings or thoughts when you read the statement, *"**I do have the million-dollar answer.**"*

Your thoughts are vital to your success, **so please do not miss this...**

I mean, WHAT IF I really do have the answers to ALL our problems, hopes, dreams, and success? I feel it could be a bestseller and help millions of people, right?

"So, what is the answer to the million-dollar WHAT-IF question?" you ask.

The answer is detailed but stay with me because the explanation is worth it!

There will be days when it will be easy to find hope, joy, happiness and promise. There will be days when it will be a little harder to find the same joy and hope, but you'll get there with some positive self-talk. Some difficult days along your life's journey may come that will make it seem nearly impossible to find hope and joy, but do not give up.

I can tell you that the million-dollar answer is NOT in any amount of money, new cars, expensive jewelry, fancy clothes, ideal lifestyles, and dream homes. In fact, I can tell you that the million-dollar answer is NOT in any worldly possession. Don't get me wrong. Having a nice home, nice cars, multiple bank accounts filled with money, good health, great friends, and family who love and support you is wonderful. Even with all these, you still will not have a perfect life and feel on top of the world every minute of every day.

As you know, I developed the *Quick-Charge* concept. I have found it to be a powerful solution to help one stay upbeat and motivated. I use it daily to lift my spirits whenever I am feeling a little drained. However, I must still find the willpower and discipline to activate the principles attached to this concept.

Think back for a moment to the story I shared about the wise teacher and the balloons. If you want to recall the whole story, please reread it again, but I will recap the emphasis of the story:

The teacher instructed each student to pick up the balloon closest to them and take it to the person whose name was written on it. Within two minutes, every child held the balloon with his or her name on it. She then explained that the balloons represent happiness. When we search for our own happiness, it is hard to find, but when we think about someone else's happiness, then everyone gets their happiness.

My late sister Sharlene embodied this concept and lifestyle. She gave everything of herself in this life to serve others and add value to people around her. She cared far more about other people's **happiness** and well-being than she did her own.

However, my sister did not have a perfect life. I am certain she did not wake up full of joy and happiness every single day.

She might have found her way there by the time she had her first cup of orange cappuccino, but I am certain she had many days that were much harder to get there than others...

Yes, I am sure my sister had some regrets along the way in life and always tried to do better. However, she continued to serve and add value to others daily. I know my sister loved others with all her heart, but still, her life was far from perfect.

I am sure my sister had plenty of WHAT-IF moments in her own life—just like you and me. But I can assure you, she impacted a lot of people and left this world better than she found it. She was a wonderful, amazing, loving, caring, optimistic, and giving woman, but she did not have it all—UNTIL she finally got to **heaven**.

What if YOU made it your goal to add value to people and serve others like Sharlene did every day of her life?

What if YOU add more value to your spouse or partner every day?

What if YOU spend more time with your children and family?

What if YOU give generously of your finances to a charity and church?

What if YOU volunteer your time to a meaningful cause?

What if YOU choose to seek the Lord and follow His leading in your life?

What if YOU finally look beyond your perceived limitations and boldly step into the life you were born to create?

Yes, **WHAT IF <u>YOU</u> while *living the life you were born to create* are the million-dollar answer to the WHAT-IF questions in life?**

Merry Christmas!

> *"You'll never change your life until you change something you do daily. The secret of your success is found in your daily routine."*
>
> – JOHN C. MAXWELL

CHAPTER 20
True Confessions

I started this book project in the early part of 2022. As I am sitting down to begin writing this chapter, it is now the beginning of 2023. I must admit, I have had plenty of ups and downs during the writing process for this book. My main challenge this past year has been my love for trading stocks. The stock market was a difficult struggle for me in 2022, and I am relatively certain that 2022 was a wild ride down for many stock traders.

Yes, 2022 was the worst year I have ever had in the markets. What's crazy is 2019–2021 were my best years ever in the markets. I had no question that I was in my zone and enjoying one of my best dreams of success in trading stocks.

How does my stock trading pertain to discovering your best dreams and living the life you were born to create?

As I have already mentioned, stock trading is one of my loves and best dreams, but 2022 was a nightmare and far from the dream I envisioned it would be. These struggles have caused me to question my trading abilities some and even put into question the direction I had planned for my dream life and stock trading.

So, I want to share the correlation to your best dreams and my stock trading struggles. My struggles made me think about all the people who have big dreams within them for living a certain life but have failed or are continually failing in their attempts to make those dreams happen. Therefore, the question is: if you fail, does that mean that your best dreams are not valid? Did you perhaps miss the boat or make a mistake? In a way, those are tricky questions, but the answers may not be so tricky.

First, I do not feel the thoughts of whether you should give up or if you have made a mistake should be one of your concerns. However, the questioning might mean that you do need to readjust your priorities, timelines, and focus.

I know how badly I want to make stock trading a regular part of my daily living and lifestyle. The schedule and timing fit in perfectly with the other best dreams I am pursuing in life. However, the trading has certainly not gone the way I had hoped this past year, and so far, 2023 is not looking very good for me either.

I have had to reevaluate what my priorities are many times along my journey to the life of which I dream. I have had to check my motives for trading this past year, and I have concluded that I have the right motives. I love trading stocks because of the challenge of playing the game. I simply love the strategy and process to work harder to get better every day.

So, the purpose of this short chapter is to offer encouragement for some of those doubts you may have as you pursue your best dreams. Just because you may not be experiencing the successes you dreamed of does not mean you are on the wrong path.

This past year has been the toughest challenge for my best dreams of stock trading daily, but I am determined to press on with my mind focused on the Lord. I am also doing my best to discern His direction for my life in this matter.

As a believer, I feel the importance of always seeking the Lord and making certain that I am not simply forcing an issue. I also feel it is healthy to question my priorities and continue to validate my best dreams. I am literally in that stage for this best dream I have for trading stocks.

Even as I am writing this book about discovering your best dreams and living the life you were born to create, I must continually be true to myself and make certain that I am practicing what I preach.

Life is a journey. I still must evaluate, readjust, and validate my best dreams at times when things are not going the way I had hoped. I am confident that I will prevail and find the answers I am seeking, but I hope these thoughts prove helpful for you to see that life does not always go as planned. However, that reversal does not mean you abandon a dream. You may simply need to readjust and approach situations differently.

> *"It is only when we take chances when our lives improve. The initial and the most difficult risk that we need to take is to become honest."*
>
> – WALTER ANDERSON

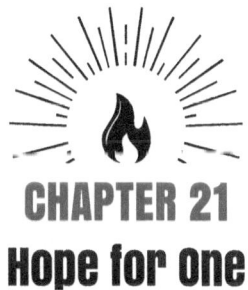

CHAPTER 21
Hope for One

As I am working on a book project, thoughts and ideas for that book often come to me in the middle of the night—just like the thought did for this chapter. That is not always convenient for me since I am normally up by 5:00 a.m. checking the news, looking at my stock charts, and readying myself for another exciting day of trading stocks in the stock market.

The thought I initially had was related mainly to the limited number of people who will reach success and the fact that those numbers dwindle even more for those who will reach the highest levels of success. My thought was this: why do I invest so much time and effort into writing a book about discovering my best dreams and living the life I was born to create when so few people will ever reach their best dream life? After all, isn't this simply a waste of my time?

> *"Never give up on a dream just because of the time it will take to accomplish it. The time will pass anyway."*
> — EARL NIGHTINGALE

If I had asked myself this question a year or so ago, I believe my answers would have been much different than they are today. When I first began writing books, my motives and priorities were different. When the idea for my first book, *Quick Charge Your Life*, first came to me, I had BIG goals and plans for my book's success.

I have never cared about being famous or making money from my writing. I just love to write, and in all honesty, I did have big ideas for the impact my books would have. I was very focused on the numbers. I had big visions and dreams to impact millions of people. I wanted my books to take off from day one and soar to the top of the charts and be read by many.

Well, my goals and dreams of reaching the top of the charts were dashed when I realized that I had little momentum or knowledge on how to promote my books. After completing my three-book series for the *Quick Charge Your Life* series, I realized that my expectations and desires were not going to measure up to my hopes.

Then I decided to tackle another topic and write about my love for stock trading and investing. I was certain that if I wrote a book on making money that I would sell thousands and thousands of copies and the messages within that book would impact many lives. However, now that I am writing my fifth book, my hopes and expectations have taken on a new thought process. Allow me to share a vision I have had many times over the years that finally answered my WHY for writing books.

This explanation will hopefully shed some light as to why I stay so inspired and driven to inspire others even though I know only a limited number of people will ever reach their full potential in life.

I have had this recurring dream or vision for many years. I have sorted through it many times, and sometimes I will get a slightly different version, but the setting and scenario are always the same.

My Vision:

I see myself on a large stage speaking with an elegant grand piano in the background. I am walking back and forth on the stage, speaking to an exceptionally large audience. It looks like I am speaking in a very large basketball arena or something. Thousands of people are in the audience, but because of the bright lights shining on the stage and in my face, all I can see are a few people in the first couple of rows.

I can make out the faces of some of my friends and family, but I do not recall who. Everyone else is in the dark, but I can see some eyes and smiles at times...

I have a headset on like most speakers wear, and the crowd is in tune with my message, hanging on every word. They are laughing, cheering, clapping, and really enjoying listening to the message.

During the vision, I will sometimes be in my body and seeing everything from the viewpoint of speaking on stage, but at times I am watching myself as a spectator off stage, as I speak. However, no matter if I am in my body or watching from the side of the stage, I can continually hear my thoughts and feel my emotions in either setting. It is so amazing!

Suddenly, I see some doors open at the very back of the room. I can see a very bright, radiant light shining through the doorway. Then the silhouette of a woman appears in the doorway, and her dress is rippling in the breeze. It seems as if she is floating into the room like an angel, but she is simply a woman walking into the auditorium, trying to quietly find a seat. She seems very timid and nervous, hoping not to draw attention to herself. However, all eyes turn their attention to her.

Then I notice that I am still standing on stage but no longer speaking. I am staring out into the crowd, and I notice that no one is looking at me any longer.

I begin peering toward the area where this woman is sitting, trying to see if I might know her. I am trying to figure out why all the attention is on her. I then sense that every single person in this room is sending love and compassion toward this one woman. I feel a warmth like I have never before felt from all the love they are sending to her.

I then see myself looking somewhat lost for words momentarily, but then I start to feel the passion to begin speaking once again, and then the vision ends.

The End of My Vision...

As I have continued to press in and sort out the meaning of this vision over the years, I believe I have finally come to realize that the Lord had uniquely led this **one** woman across my path that night so that she might hear the message.

He had given me something to share so that **one** person could hear it. The only key role that I played in this vision was that He was using me to deliver the message to that **one** person.

I was reminded that God would do everything He has done just for **me** alone. Because He is omnipotent and omnipresent, He would likewise do everything He has done for me just for **you** as well.

So, I share this vision because my mindset has now changed since I first started writing books, and I feel my vision will help you to adjust your priorities as well.

Whenever I now write and publish a new book, my hope is to reach at least one person. If only one person reads my book and finds some value, causing that one person to be inspired enough to look beyond his or her perceived limitations and boldly step into the life he or she was born to create, then my mission has been accomplished for that book project.

Yes, if the thoughts, ideas, and messages that the Lord inspires me to write in each book I publish can reach at least one person and add value to that person's life, then, my friend, I have done my job. I can go to sleep with peace in my heart and a smile on my face.

Perhaps you think that is a terribly low bar to set for myself. Well, yes, I did feel this way when the thought first came to be, but I realized it is out of my hands as to the number of people who will or won't be impacted.

The fact is, I only have control over one aspect and that is in acting upon my best dreams. So, hoping for at least one life to be changed is a BIG goal and far greater than leaving my dreams of writing behind and not giving it a chance to reach anyone. The same is true for your dreams as well!

> *"If you let your best dreams pass you by then you have a **ZERO** percent chance of its happening."*
>
> – TOMMY TURNER

So, if for only one person, I would begin the process all over again of authoring a new book, spending hours and hours researching and studying. I would work well into the night listening to podcasts, reading interesting articles, reading through inspirational books, and listening to audio books. If this book was only for one person, I would spend multiple days, weeks, and months compiling all my thoughts, ideas, and recording my findings. If for only one person, I would dig even deeper as I searched for appropriate quotes, Scriptures, reading back over past journal notes, and continuing to pray for direction throughout the entire process!

Yes, if all my hard work could add value and change at least one person's life, I would do it all over again and again. That is one of my best dreams, and I am living it every day. Perhaps one day, someone like yourself will read one of my books and be inspired enough to go out and change the world, inspire others, and add value to millions of lives. Then my book would reach millions, but for now, my focus is on **one**.

What is the correlation between my vision, this book, and your best dreams?

I have a hope that at least one person will read my book and be changed by the messages within that book, but I do still have HIGH expectations. However, my focus is only on conveying the messages that the Lord wants me to write.

Perhaps the following thought will clarify this last point a little better: the main difference between expectation and hope is that **expectations usually depend on someone, while hopes do not**. Expectations and hopes are beliefs or wishes about the future. An *expectation* is "a strong belief in the future," while *hope* is "a feeling of optimism or a wish for something to happen."

You see, my hope is to add value to at least one person and inspire that person to look beyond his or her perceived limitations and boldly step into the life he or she was born to create. Still, I have no control over whether someone will choose to purchase one of my books or if it will help one person or one million.

My best dreams when authoring a new book do start with the hope of touching at least one life. I have HIGH expectations, NO limitations, and unknown destinations. However, my goal is simply to act on my dream and write the book. The rest is in the Lord's hands. If my book does add value to at least one person, then it did what I had hoped for, but how few or how many people are touched by my book is not my call.

This additional illustration might help drive this point home even more: when a woman is "expecting" a child, she has hopes for a healthy baby. However, her expectation is not a guarantee of success. You can have hopes, dreams, and high expectations, but you do not control the ultimate outcome. However, that end result should not diminish your passion and drive to chase after your best dreams!

My drive and passions are elevated when I write and publish a book and pursue my best dreams. The incredible and satisfying feeling of joy I have when I recall my vision of delivering a message that helped change someone's life is what keeps me driving toward more successes.

I may never know if a book I write has any positive impact on anyone who reads it, but what I do know is this: **if I do not put in the effort and act on my best dreams, then no one will ever get the opportunity to read my books.** I am motivated by the fact that if I never write and publish a book, I would have absolutely no chance of accomplishing my best dream.

The same goes for whatever best dreams you may have. If you do nothing about them, then your best dreams will eventually pass you by. If you continue to wait, instead of acting on your best dreams, then you will never know what could've been. Sadly, far too many dreams go to the grave unrealized.

> *"Dare to dream, but even more importantly, dare to put action behinds your dreams."*
> — Josh Hinds

This book and this chapter may not help anyone, or it may help a few people, or it may help several people to find the drive to look beyond their perceived limitations and boldly step into the life they were born to create.

However, the numbers should not matter. Should you choose to pursue a certain career, your best dreams should not be determined by how much money you might make. Your best dreams should not be motivated by how many people you think you can help.

Your best dreams should not be motivated by how your dreams will help you get to something or someplace better than where you are now.

Yes, your best dreams should have HIGH expectations, NO limitations, but the destinations will be determined by the Lord as you allow Him to lead.

The ONLY thing your best dreams should have right now is enough hope and conviction that the thought of **NOT** chasing after your goals and dreams, causes you to ignite a fire within to rise out of your chair and begin to put a plan into action in order to accomplish it.

This next thought is powerful, so please read it a few times. You don't want to miss this truth!

If you fail, then adjust and try again. If you fail again, then adjust and try again. If you fail again, then adjust some more and try again. If you fail again, then adjust a little more and try again. If you fail again, then readjust and try again. If you fail again, then readjust a bit more and try again. If you fail again, then adjust a little more and try again.

Some might see this continual readjusting as a total failure and even crazy, but trying again is far from crazy and NOT failure. It is MUCH better to have tried and tried again and fail multiple times than never to try at all.

However, here is the answer to your best dreams and the point you absolutely **MUST** understand: if after you fail multiple times, you still have the fire and determination to get back up, readjust, and keep pressing on to achieve a dream, then I want to say congratulations in advance!

When you reach this level of commitment and determination, then you have discovered one of your **best dreams,** and something wonderful is going to happen. You have found your path to success!

"Take action. An inch of movement will bring you closer to your goals than a mile of intention."

– STEVE MARABOLI

"You don't have to be great to start, but you have to start to be great."

– ZIG ZIGLAR

conclusion

When I write a book, I always base the subject matter on something that I am currently living through and or have gone through in the past. I have spent time discovering information and insights that I feel would be valuable to share with others in hopes to add some value to those who read it. Thus is the case for this book. I am continually discovering and validating my best dreams and looking beyond my perceived limitations to boldly step into the life I was born to create. Verifying my best dreams is an ongoing process for me as it is for everyone else as well.

You may be searching for the ideal career that fits who you are. You may be looking to improve other areas of your life to find the *you* that you know you were born to create. Whatever the case may be, the process is ongoing.

As I was contemplating my message for the conclusion of this book. I had one more thought that brought on another chapter and helped me write the conclusion for this book as well. I would like to share the significance and uniqueness of the thought that birthed a new chapter.

I honestly thought my manuscript for this book was concluded and ready to send off to the editors. However, another thought occurred to me, and I realized I had one more important chapter to write which became chapter nine about discovering how you are wired.

The thought for a new chapter was so important to me because the WHAT-IF chapter was originally chapter 18, but I REALLY wanted it to be chapter 19 to honor my late sister Sharlene. When the WHAT-IF chapter was originally written and placed as chapter 18 in the flow chart, I was okay with leaving it as chapter 18, but I really wanted it to be chapter 19. At the time, the chapter simply did not fit in the flow chart of the book until the idea for a new chapter changed all of that.

Now, the reason number 19 was so important to me regarding the WHAT-IF chapter and my sister was because she passed away on January **19**, 2007. Literally as I was writing the date and year my sister passed, I realized that if you add the 2 + 7 as in 200Z, the year she passed, those two numbers add up to **9,** which is the number of the new chapter I added at the last minute to make it all come together. That discovery gave me another *Quick Charge*!

Her passing was such a shock and brought about a significant change in my life, altering my life and the lives of many others in a very compelling way. The day she passed, I felt this burden to do all that I could to honor her life and do my best to be even the slightest version of who she was as a person.

As I have already shared, Sharlene was ALL about adding value and serving others. She would go out of her way to do things for others. I will never understand why God called her home so early in life, but I know His plans are far greater than mine. Still, her homegoing has always left a question in my heart.

When she passed, I had not yet written any of my books nor had I discovered many of the incredible successes I enjoy today. I am certain that she would look past all my faults and mistakes and be so incredibly proud of all that I have accomplished since her passing.

I am convinced that if she were still on this earth today, she would've read every single one of my books multiple times by now and promoted them to the world. Knowing her, she would've gone on Amazon and purchased a few hundred copies to get my book sales off to a good start...not because she felt my books were brilliant or any better than any others, but simply because she loved me. But then, she would have done that for any of her family or friends. My sister loved people, and she loved adding value to others.

I really trust that this book added value to your life and inspired you to realize that you are unique, and you were born for greatness. *My life's vision is to inspire individuals to realize their uniqueness, discover their dreams, and thrive in this lifetime.*

God does not make mistakes. Unfortunately, people do make mistakes and can really mess up at times, but the Lord has a plan for your life regardless of your past mistakes. If you will press in and look beyond your perceived limitations and boldly step into the life YOU were born to create, you will be living your BEST dreams.

> *"Don't be pushed around by the fears in your mind. Be led by the dreams in your heart."*
> – ROY T. BENNETT

> *"A year from now you will wish you had started today."*
> – KAREN LAMB

contact

For more information about the *quick-charge* book series,
please visit us on the web at http://quickchargeyourlife.com.
To learn more about the author, Tommy Turner,
visit http://tommyturner.com

www.ingramcontent.com/pod-product-compliance
Lightning Source LLC
Chambersburg PA
CBHW021643120626
46545CB00002B/675